Dedication

for

OUR PARENTS,
Ruth Phillips
Robert and Barbara Gstohl

OUR HUSBANDS,
Jim Peeples
Rob Seabury

AND OUR CHILDREN
Jim, Chuck, and Bob Peeples
Katie and Barbara Seabury

Ready-to-Use Science Activities for the Elementary Classroom

Debra Seabury
Susan Peeples

**THE CENTER FOR APPLIED
RESEARCH IN EDUCATION**
West Nyack, New York 10994

Library of Congress Cataloging-in-Publication Data

Seabury, Debra.
    Ready-to-use science activities for the elementary
classroom.
    ISBN 0-87628-743-7
    1. Science—Study and teaching (Elementary)—United
States—Handbooks, manuals, etc.   I. Peeples, Susan.
II. Title.
LB1585.3.S43   1987   86-31704
372.3'5044   CIP

Printed in the United States of America

20   19   18   17   16   15

ISBN 0-87628-743-7

**THE CENTER FOR APPLIED RESEARCH
IN EDUCATION**
West Nyack, NY 10994
A Simon & Schuster Company

On the World Wide Web at http://www.phdirect.com

Prentice Hall International (UK) Limited, *London*
Prentice Hall of Australia Pty. Limited, *Sydney*
Prentice Hall Canada Inc., *Toronto*
Prentice Hall Hispanoamericana, S.A., *Mexico*
Prentice Hall of India Private Limited, *New Delhi*
Prentice Hall of Japan, Inc., *Tokyo*
Simon & Schuster Asia Pte. Ltd., *Singapore*
Editora Prentice Hall do Brasil, Ltda., *Rio de Janeiro*

About the Authors

DEBRA SEABURY earned her B.A. degree from Western Washington University, majoring in elementary education with an English minor. She has taught grades 4 through 6.

SUSAN PEEPLES also received her B.A. degree from Western Washington University, where she majored in elementary education with minors in art and library science. She has taught grades 1 through 6 as well as serving as a remedial specialist in both reading and math.

With over 20 years' combined experience in the elementary classroom, the authors are currently teaching in the Ferndale (Washington) Public Schools, where both have done work on the development of goals and curriculum. They have also been writing together for four years, during which time several of their articles have appeared in *OASIS* magazine.

CONTENTS

About This Resource

Ready-to-Use Science Activities for the Elementary Classroom offers classroom teachers practical materials for teaching science content while reinforcing basic skills. Designed to stimulate interest, these interdisciplinary activities give elementary students practice in reading, math, and writing skills while helping them to understand the life and earth sciences.

Developed by two teachers with over 20 years' combined teaching experience, these activities are clearly written and easy to use. Each activity is complete and ready for immediate use by students for discovery and review.

Ready-to-Use Science Activities for the Elementary Classroom is organized into four sections.

- "Section One: For the Teacher" includes science bulletin board suggestions, project ideas for art and creative writing, and full-page forms, calendars, and science certificates of merit.

- "Section Two: Life Science Activities" is divided into three units—Plants, Animals, and Human Body. Each unit offers reproducible activity sheets for your students, covering such topics as "Seed Distribution," "Plant Graph," "Sea Turtles," "Animal Families," "Your Brain," and "Germs."

- "Section Three: Earth Science Activities" is centered around Geology, Weather, and Space. Your students are introduced to such topics as "Magnetism," "The Water Cycle," and "Early Astronomers" through a variety of activities including word searches and crossword puzzles.

- "Section Four: Answer Key" provides all of the answers to the activity sheets in Sections Two and Three.

These sections offer you great flexibility in selecting materials for a six-week study of the life sciences, for example, or a three-week plants unit, or a one-week concentration on mammals. Because all of the activities are laid out for you step-by-step, you can quickly plan and prepare your lessons, saving yourself valuable time for quality instruction.

Through the variety of suggested activities and experiences in *Ready-to-Use Science Activities for the Elementary Classroom*, you can lead your students through a wide range of concepts and discoveries. Students will grow in their understanding of plants, animals, the earth, and themselves.

Debra Seabury

Susan Peeples

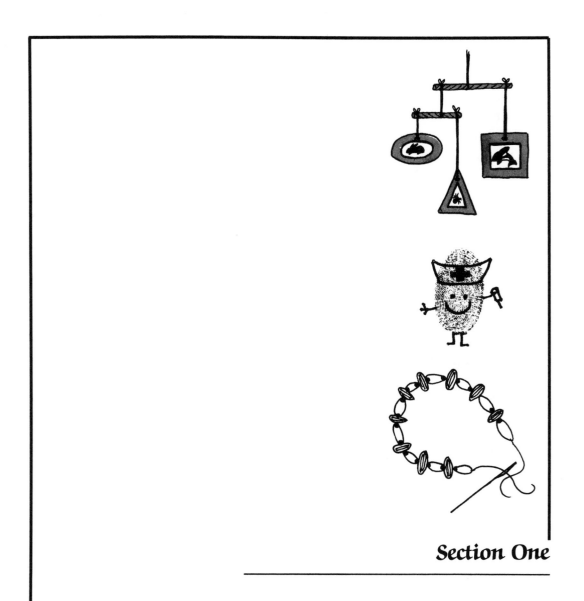

Section One

FOR THE TEACHER

Take a moment to look at this book and to get a feel for its content and structure. *Ready-to-Use Science Activities for the Elementary Classroom* is divided into four sections:

- Section One is for the teacher and includes teacher aides and teacher-directed activities
- Sections Two and Three are for the student and contain student activity pages
- Section Four offers a complete answer key to the activity pages

Let's take a closer look at each part of this book.

TEACHER AIDS

The teacher aids begin with two forms. The resources form is an organizational tool enabling you to keep a current list of "extras." Each time you teach your units, you have only to add new resources. These listings eliminate searching for names, numbers, and titles each time you use your units. In compiling your lists, be sure to check public libraries as well as your school's resource center. Government agencies and professional organizations are also good sources.

The calendar page is for planning and scheduling your units. Reproduce as many pages as necessary. After looking over the material and your completed resources list, select the lessons, activities, and resources that best meet your objectives. Begin filling in your calendar. Don't forget to schedule films and guests well in advance.

Bulletin boards are excellent teaching tools, and those suggested here reinforce the content of these science activities. They can be easily copied by using an opaque or overhead projector. Of course, you can adapt the ideas to your space and available materials.

TEACHER-DIRECTED ACTIVITIES

The teacher-directed activities and art projects are integral to each section of this book. These concrete activities reinforce the content of each unit while leading to new discoveries. Art lessons and activities get students actively involved with learning, so use as many as your scheduling allows.

The themes of this book are expanded through creative writing. These lessons explore beyond the basic science content and stretch the students' imagination and creativity. Each creative writing activity is complete with reproducible pages for the presentation of the students' final work.

All too often, units have a way of "fizzling out." Culminations and student awards keep interest high right up to the last days of your science units. Everyone is left with positive feelings of accomplishment.

GETTING STUDENTS STARTED

The student part of *Ready-to-Use Science Activities* has two sections: Life Science and Earth Science. These sections further divide into six units—plants, animals, human body, geology, weather, and space. Each unit includes similar types of materials that are discussed in detail below.

Vocabulary

Three types of activities to introduce and expand vocabulary are used in this book.

- Word searches expose students to new vocabulary specific to the sciences.
- Crossword puzzles develop and reinforce vocabulary.
- Handwriting pages provide handwriting practice but also reinforce vocabulary and develop spelling skills.

These handwriting pages can also be used for recording definitions or writing sentences.

Reading

This book uses three reading formats. The modified cloze activities give students information and practice in context word analysis. The student chooses the best word from the listed choices. Comprehension pages with accompanying illustrations also cover basic science content. They address a variety of learning styles by challenging children to understand visually displayed information.

The "ready, set, go" selections are readings about interesting or unusual topics related to the specific unit topics. Each of these "ready, set, go" pages has a prereading activity, the reading itself, and comprehension checks. Whenever possible, expand the interest these selections create by displaying related items or additional readings.

Math

The math lessons included in this book are based on the content of each unit. These lessons emphasize basic operations. They are not designed to introduce new math skills, but rather encourage students to exercise logic and reason in problem solving.

Puzzles

A variety of puzzle formats give students opportunities to encounter information in new and interesting ways. Use these puzzles with your whole class, small groups, or with individual students. Puzzles also work well in activity centers or as homework assignments to be shared with parents.

Quick Checks

Ready-to-Use Science Activities uses quick checks for review and evaluation. Each of the six units concludes with a one-page review of the material specific to that unit. These quick checks may also be combined for evaluation of an entire section or used for review practice.

Resources

Audio-Visuals (films, filmstrips, etc.)

number   *title*

_____   _____

_____   _____

_____   _____

_____   _____

_____   _____

_____   _____

Books (magazines, prints, transparencies, etc.)

title   *author/publisher*

_____   _____

_____   _____

_____   _____

_____   _____

_____   _____

_____   _____

Speakers-Field Trips-Others

_____

_____

_____

Planning Calendar

MONDAY	TUESDAY	WEDNESDAY	THURSDAY	FRIDAY

Life Science Bulletin Boards

"Parts of a Seed, Plant, and Flower" is to be used with the plant unit. For maximum student participation, make vocabulary cards. Students can then attach them with push pins. Provide a key for self-checking.

For "Classifying Critters," you will need to make animal cards for the pockets. Students remove cards and place them in the appropriate groups. Again you may want to provide for self-checking.

To make "Body Match," enlarge the boy and girl silhouettes on black paper. Mount on background. Make a set of body part word cards on cloud shapes. Choose vocabulary appropriate for your grade level. Using push pins and heavy yarn, students connect words to the correct body parts.

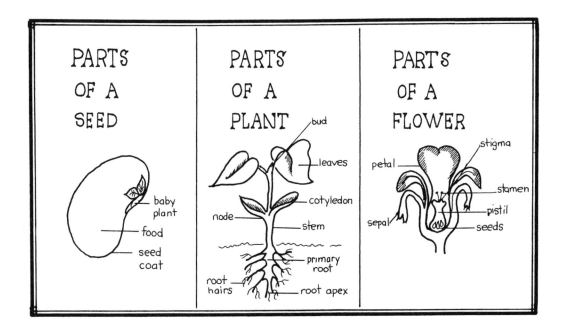

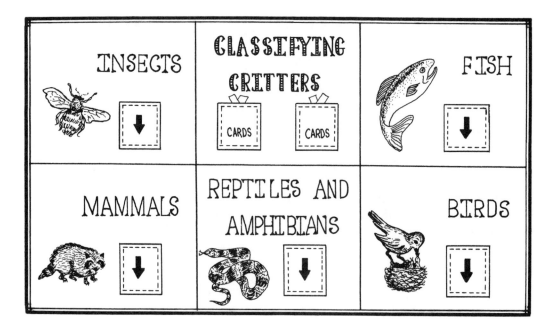

Life Science Art Projects

Seed Necklaces

To make these necklaces, you will need needles, heavy duty thread, and a variety of seeds. Large, tough seeds, such as pumpkin or squash seeds, work well. If the seeds are quite hard, soak them in water for several hours to soften. For variety of color, seeds can be dyed in a solution of food coloring and water.

String necklaces by pushing the needle through each seed. Seeds can be strung lengthwise or by one end as well as through their centers. Repeated patterns or designs are especially attractive. Be sure to tie off the ends securely.

Animal Mobiles

This activity will teach students about balance and geometry as well as animals. You will need drawing paper, glue, colored paper cut into geometric shapes, and straws.

Have students draw animal pictures, cut them out, and glue to colored shapes. On the back of each shape, write the name of the animal and, perhaps, the group to which it belongs. Assemble the mobiles using straws and yarn. You may need to adjust for balance before hanging.

Instead of drawing, students could cut pictures from magazines. Drawings might also be done on acetate to create a "stained glass" effect. Students could also work in small groups making mobiles for each animal or mammal group.

Silhouettes

 To make silhouettes of your students, attach black paper to a chalkboard. Have a student stand near the paper. Use an overhead projector to create the silhouette shadow. Adjust distances for clarity. Trace the silhouette with chalk. Repeat for each student. Cut out silhouettes and mount on contrasting paper. Complete the project by allowing students to add words cut from magazines that they feel describe themselves. For fun, display numbered silhouettes and have students guess their classmates. You may want to include a few other silhouettes such as your own, your school's principal, or famous people as well.

Fingerprint Art

Simple fingerprint art makes effective decorations for cards, stationery, or note pads. You will need stamp pads and fine-point, felt-tip pens. Press one finger onto the stamp pad and print on practice paper. Prints may be vertical or horizontal. Experiment. Use pens to add details. Simple cartooning books will offer suggestions for expressions and details. Allow students plenty of time for practice. Select favorites and stamp finished copies. These simple projects make clever thank-you notes for classroom visitors and field trip sponsors. (Hint: People, insects, and animals make especially good subjects.)

Life Science Creative Writing

Green Thumb Seed Company

For this activity's packet and seed, write final copies on the seed shape patterns, cut out, and fasten together. Color, cut, and paste the packet. A drawing of the student's plant completes the packet. Share stories in a reading center along with a book about plants or display stories in the school library.

My Animal Report

This activity enables students to complete beginning level reports. To avoid concentration on "favorite" subjects, make a list of possibilities. Have students draw subjects from a hat, or assign animals. If students feel strongly about favorites, allow them to complete additional reports. Students can easily present their reports orally by reading only their answers. Encourage students to share pictures and books about their animals as well.

People Analogies

Foot is to person as paw is to dog.

 is to 🐤 as 💪 is to ☺.

"People Analogies" focuses students on common relationships in a unique way. Brainstorm many of these with your class. Use the sentence frame, _____ is to _____ as _____ is to _____. Comparisons between people and animals work particularly well. Have students choose their favorite analogies to illustrate using rhebus pictures for their final work.

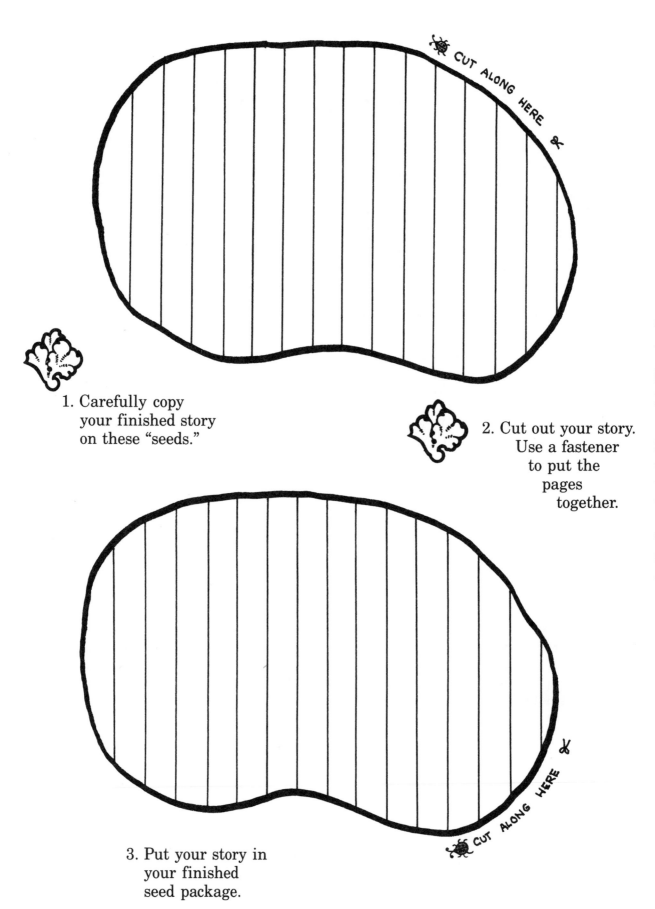

CUT ALONG HERE ✂

1. Carefully copy
   your finished story
   on these "seeds."

2. Cut out your story.
   Use a fastener
   to put the
   pages
   together.

CUT ALONG HERE ✂

3. Put your story in
   your finished
   seed package.

THUMB

GREEN
SEED COMPANY

MANUFACTURED BY:

paste

fold

Plant name:

How to plant:

This plant will
grow to be:

CUT AROUND THE OUTSIDE EDGE

Name _____

My Animal Report on _____

Use an encyclopedia and other books to help answer each question. Use complete sentences. Proofread your work.

1. What is your animal's name? _____

_____

2. To what group does your animal belong? _____

_____

3. In what part of the world does your animal live? _____

_____

_____

4. Describe what your animal looks like. _____

_____

_____

_____

5. What is your animal's home like? _____

_____

_____

6. What does your animal eat? _____

_____

_____

7. Tell about the young animals. What are they called? What is their family like?

_____

_____

_____

8. Who are your animal's natural enemies? How does it protect itself? _____

_____

_____

_____

9. How long does your animal usually live? _____

_____

_____

_____

10. Complete these sentences.

One interesting thing I learned about _____ was

_____

Another interesting thing about _____ was _____

_____

But the most interesting thing of all about _____ was

_____

Bibliography:

Name of encyclopedia, "Name of Article," Volume, page number

_____

_____

Author, Name of Book, date, page number.

1. _____

_____

_____

2. _____

_____

_____

On another paper, draw a picture of your animal.

People Analogies

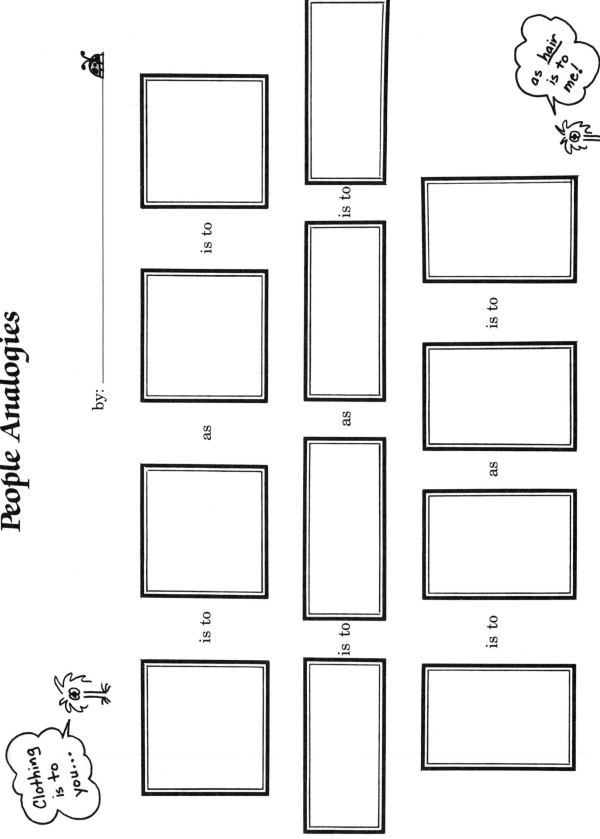

Life Science Activities

Dissecting a Plant

For this activity, you will need a sharp knife and a plant for each pair or small group of students. Small bedding plants such as marigolds or pansies are good choices. Slightly dry plants work best and create less mess. You will also need paper towels for collecting the dirt and for clean-up.

Have students carefully remove their plants from the soil. Remove the loose dirt by gently shaking the plant over a paper towel. Examine the plant parts. Cut a flower in half to examine the internal parts. On a paper divided in half, students can record their findings. On one half draw and label the plant. The flower goes on the other half. You may want to list vocabulary on the board.

Gathered Gardens

For "Gathered Gardens," you will need three pie pans, three soil samples, three large plastic bags, and rubber bands or twist ties.

Gather your soil samples from different locations, such as the roadside, beach, or playground. Spread the soils in the pie pans and sprinkle gently with water. Place each garden in a plastic bag and close with a band or twist tie.

Label each garden as to where the soil was gathered and place them in a sunny window.

Check the gardens daily. Look for new plants. Compare gardens. Identify as many plants as possible.

Mounting Insects

You will need the following materials for "Mounting Insects": dead insects, cigar or shoe boxes, styrofoam to line the bottoms of the boxes, long straight pins, felt-tipped markers, and slips of paper.

Collect several small dead insects. Stick a straight pin through the thorax of each insect, then into the styrofoam-lined box. Identify and label the insects. The collections can be safely carried home by simply closing the lid.

Clean, Cook, and Eat a Fish

To do this with your class, you will need a sharp knife, cooking supplies, and a fresh whole fish. Unless you can catch one yourself, check with a fish market or grocery store's meat/fish department well in advance. Begin by examining the fish. Locate the external parts. Use the knife to scrape off the scales. Cut behind the gills to remove the head. Examine the gills. Cut back from the throat along the midline of the belly. Expose the internal parts for examination. Wash and scrape the cavity. Split the fish by cutting along the backbone. Note the bone structure. Check a cookbook for specific cooking instructions. Enjoy!

Pulse Rates

Your students can feel the strong beating of their hearts by checking pulse rates. Begin by placing the tips of the fingers on the artery along the side of the wrist. Children 7 to 10 years old should have a rate between 70 and 115 beats per minute. Compute rates by counting beats for 6 seconds and then multiplying by 10.

You can actually "see" the moving pulse by pressing a thin strip of posterboard or a paper match onto a thumb tack and placing the head of the tack against your wrist.

You may want children to chart or graph their different pulse rates. Have them check rates resting and after various levels of exercise.

Let's Visit a Hospital

A hospital visit helps students to understand that hospitals are not only concerned with sick or injured people, but also with promoting good health.

Contact the public relations person or administrative office of your community hospital to make arrangements for your tour. Most hospitals offer tours of such areas as pediatrics, X-ray, physical therapy, and their pharmacy. Many will also allow students to view newborn babies in the nursery. If your class has a special area of interest, be sure to ask in advance.

Tours are often run by hospital volunteers. Remember that "thank you" messages are always appreciated.

Wrapping Up Life Science

On the final day of life science study you will be sending home students' completed work. To make the culmination of your work really special, plan a lunch and invite parents or other special guests. Emphasize plant and animal foods such as peanut butter, sprouts, or even chocolate milk from the cocoa plant and the cow! Have students explain or demonstrate projects, bulletin boards, and centers. Display children's art. Share stories and reports. Award student certificates. For a perfect finishing touch, order flowers delivered to you and your class with congratulations for a job well done.

Life Science Degree

awarded to

_____

Be it known to all that this person is awarded this special degree for meritorious work in Life Science.

Congratulations!

signed: _____

date: _____

Earth Science Bulletin Boards

Make "Periods in Time" by covering the entire board with blue and adding green for land. Divide into eras. Have students draw creatures and place them in the appropriate eras.

For "Today's Weather" you will need to prepare cards for major cities and sky conditions (cloudy, sunny, and so forth) Students can make new temperature cards each day. Students should place the cards each day to reflect current weather conditions.

Make rocket-shaped cards for "Traveling in Space." Students match cards to the appropriate planet. One card set should be planet names. Another might be numbered to correspond to the order from the sun. Still others could carry attributes such as "most moons," or "closest to the sun."

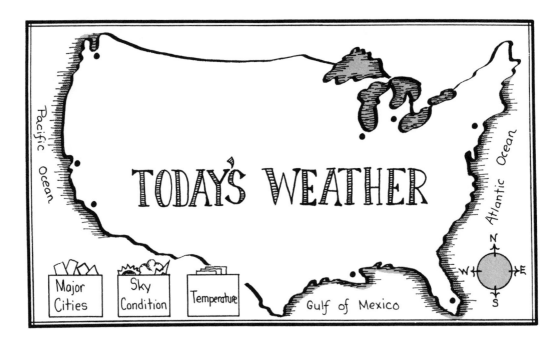

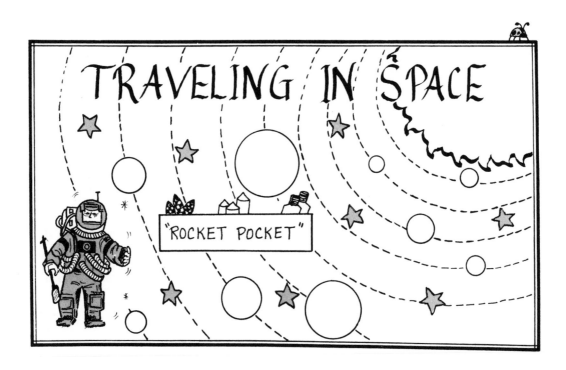

Earth Science Art Projects

Earth Painting

This activity is best done outdoors, where you will find your materials. In addition to natural objects, you will need large drawing paper. The paintings are done by rubbing leaves, dirt, stones, or what-have-you on the paper. Experimenting is the key. Try anything that looks interesting. Flowers, berries, and bark give a variety of colors. Results may be realistic pictures or free-form designs. Try displaying them on a background of natural burlap.

Making Fossils

For making fossils, you will need foil pans, clay, plaster of Paris, and small objects to "fossilize" such as bones, shells, or even hands! Flatten about 1 inch of clay into the bottom of the pan. Press objects into the clay, then remove them from the clay. Pour plaster of Paris into the pan and allow it to harden. Remove pan and clay to reveal your fossil.

Spacescapes

Very interesting "spacescapes" can be done using black paper and colored chalk or pastels. Brainstorm to generate ideas for bizarre creatures and strange plants. Have artists sign their work with white crayon. Spray pictures with hairspray or commercial fixative to minimize smearing. Mat with complementary pastels (bright mats detract from the artwork) and display on a dark background.

Earth Science Creative Writing

The Magic Stone

For magic stone stories, give each child a small stone (polished, if possible). Discuss the magical quality of their stones for transporting them back through time. Brainstorm historic and prehistoric periods, interesting words and situations. Allow children to develop their ideas in rough form, and then proofread and recopy in final form on the worksheet. Bind into a class book for display.

Weather Haiku

A simple way to write weather haiku is to choose a subject and divide it into three parts, one for each line. A standard haiku form has three lines. Line one has five syllables. Line two has seven syllables and line three has five syllables. Do several poems together before students work individually to create their own haiku poems on the worksheet.

Here is an example:

THUNDER

(5) Rolling and rumbling	(sound)
(7) Dark black clouds bumping the sky	(size)
(5) Bringing lightning's bright flash	(action)

A Letter from Space

This activity will enable students to write friendly letters about their unusual adventures. Students imagine trips to distant planets. In letters to their friends back home, encourage children to describe details of their trips, hosts, and destinations. You may want to extend the lesson by addressing envelopes and designing "space stamps."

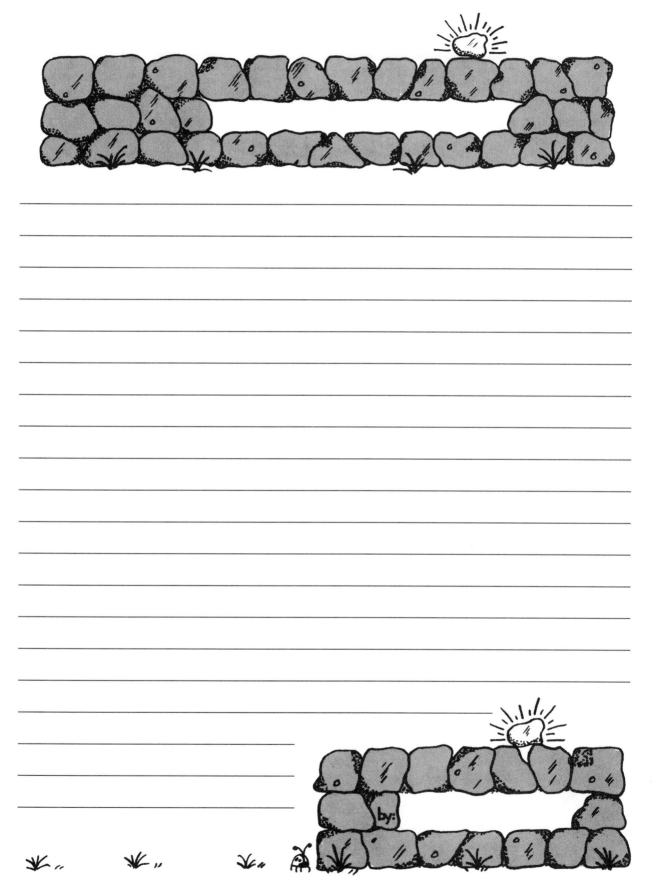

Write your Haiku
poems on the lines.
Cut out and mount
on colored paper. Add
a picture if you
wish.

_____
_____
_____

_____
_____
_____
_____
_____
_____
_____
_____
_____
_____
_____
_____

_____
_____

Earth Science Activities

Sedimentary Sandwiches

To make sedimentary sandwiches, you will need at least three types of bread and several fillings. Using a variety of textures, such as jelly, banana slices, and chunky peanut butter best illustrates actual rock layers. Build sandwiches using half slices of bread and as many fillings as you choose. Discuss the formation of sedimentary rock. You may also bend your sandwiches to show folded mountains or cut them to illustrate block mountains. You can do a passable metamorphosis by squeezing, but have plenty of napkins ready! Complete by consuming your experiment.

Making Rain

You can make rain in your classroom. You will need metal cans, ice, bowls, rulers, and warm water. Fill a can with ice. Set a ruler across the rim of a bowl of warm water. Carefully place the can on the ruler. Wait and watch. Warm water vapor rises from the bowl and comes into contact with the cold metal of the can. The water vapor condenses and "rains" back into the bowl. This activity actually creates a miniature water cycle. Ask students to relate their experiment to our earth's natural water cycle.

Parachute Fun

Children can learn about air pressure by making parachutes. You will need string, handkerchief, and small weights such as erasers. Tie a piece of string to each corner of a handkerchief. Gather the other ends of the strings and secure to a small weight. To use your parachute, set the weight in the center of the handkerchief, gather together, and toss into the air. Watch the pressure of the air hold the parachute up. Compare to a weight tossed without a parachute. Try indoor and outdoor launches. Discuss variables such as wind, weight, and size of chute.

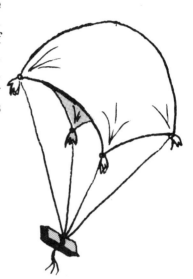

What Would You Take?

This is a discussion activity with many possibilities. Begin by having students list the things they would want to take along with them on a space flight. Each person then chooses the ten things from his or her own list that are most important. Group students in pairs. Each pair now merges their lists and chooses the ten most important things. Join pairs to form groups of four or six. Again the group must combine lists and choose the ten items most important for their space flight. You may want to end with a class discussion of what was chosen and why.

Gym Solar System

To help students visualize the relative distances of our solar system, you can create a gym solar system. You will need a large space at least 80 feet in length (a gym is perfect). You will also need information cards for the nine planets. You may want to include distance from the sun, the number of moons, or other information on these cards along with the planet names. Starting with a wall to represent the surface of the sun, use the chart below to measure the distance to each planet. Have a child hold the appropriate card and stand for each planet. You may want children to work in groups to do the measuring and placing of each planet.

In this model the Earth would be about the size of a cantaloupe.

Planet	Actual Average Distance	Model Distance
MERCURY	36,000,000 mi	9″
VENUS	67,000,000 mi.	1′5″
EARTH	93,000,000 mi.	2′
MARS	141,000,000 mi.	3′1″
JUPITER	483,000,000 mi.	10′6″
SATURN	888,000,000 mi.	19′3″
URANUS	1,779,000,000 mi.	38′8″
NEPTUNE*	2,788,000,000 mi.	60′7″
PLUTO*	3,658,000,000 mi.	79′6″

*Pluto is usually farther from the sun than Neptune, but not always.

Wrapping Up Earth Sciences

Upon completion of the earth science unit, you will have a collection of booklets and tests, writing activities, and art projects. Children derive great personal satisfaction from seeing all of their efforts gathered together into a folder that can be taken proudly home and shared with families. Make folders by folding a 12″x18″ sheet of construction paper and taping or stapling the sides. Glue awards on the fronts of the folders and you are set to put all materials inside. Gold self-adhesive stars and special seals add a nice touch. Layered (sedimentary) cookies or "rock candy" would be a perfect treat as children head home with their folders.

YOUR WONDERFUL WORLD...

PRESENTED TO: _____

FOR COMPLETING THE STUDY OF GEOLOGY, WEATHER & SPACE

Signed: _____   Date: _____

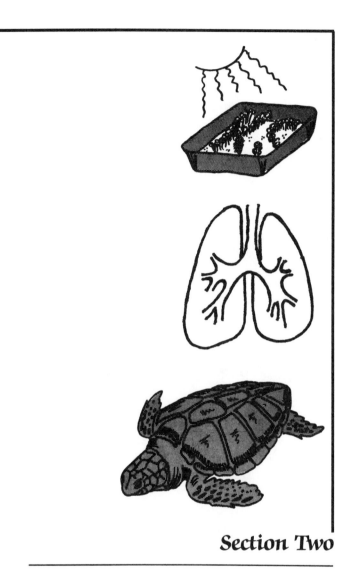

Section Two

LIFE SCIENCE
ACTIVITIES

Seeds Word Search

Look for each of these words in the word search. The words can be found either across or down.

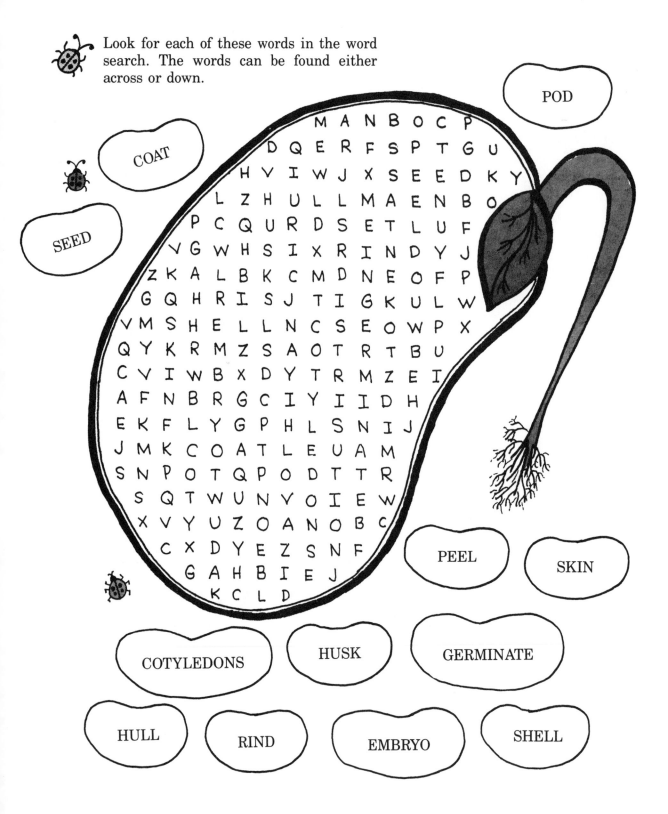

POD

COAT

SEED

```
        M A N B O C P
      D Q E R F S P T G U
    H V I W J X S E E D K Y
    L Z H U L L M A E N B O
    P C Q U R D S E T L U F
    V G W H S I X R I N D Y J
    Z K A L B K C M D N E O F P
    G Q H R I S J T I G K U L W
    V M S H E L L N C S E O W P X
    Q Y K R M Z S A O T R T B U
    C V I W B X D Y T R M Z E I
    A F N B R G C I Y I I D H
    E K F L Y G P H L S N I J
    J M K C O A T L E U A M
    S N P O T Q P O D T T R
      S Q T W U N V O I E W
      X V Y U Z O A N O B C
      C X D Y E Z S N F
        G A H B I E J
          K C L D
```

PEEL

SKIN

COTYLEDONS

HUSK

GERMINATE

HULL

RIND

EMBRYO

SHELL

Seeds

A seed is really a baby plant and some food in a protective seed coat. The baby plant is called the embryo. It needs the stored food to grow on until it can make its own food.

Seeds come in all sizes and shapes. Avocados have large seeds. A coconut is the largest of all seeds. Some seeds are as small as grains of sand. Poppy seeds are this small. Seeds from an orchid plant are so tiny that they look like dust. They are the smallest of seeds.

When a seed germinates or begins to grow, it uses the stored food to grow. First, a root grows from one end of the seed. Later, a sprout begins to grow and pushes up through the soil. The first thick leaves are called cotyledons. They help the young plant to produce food.

Most plants grow from seeds, and later they produce seeds to grow still more mature plants.

Use a dictionary to help you define these words:

1. embryo _____

_____

_____

2. sprout _____

_____

_____

3. cotyledons _____

_____

_____

4. germinate _____

_____

_____

Corn and Beans

Corn Seed: Study the parts.

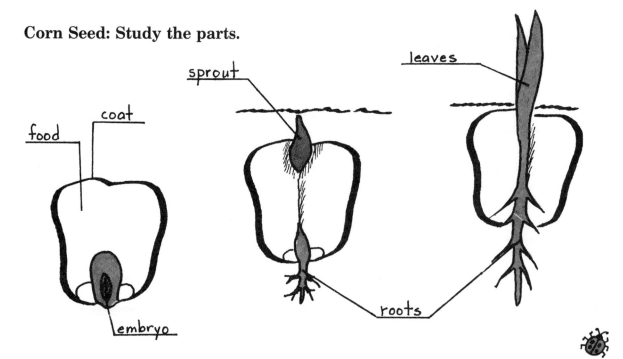

food
coat
sprout
leaves
embryo
roots

Bean Seed: Label *coat, food, embryo, root, leaves,* and *cotyledons.*

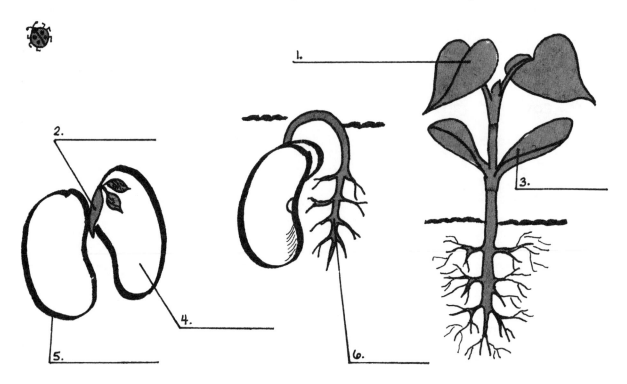

1.
2.
3.
4.
5.
6.

Name ―――――――――――――――

Sprout Letters

You can "grow" your own initials in alfalfa sprouts if you follow a few simple steps. You will need a wash cloth, a shallow pan, plastic wrap, newspaper, and, of course, alfalfa seeds.

Begin by soaking the seeds in water for about an hour. Then dampen the cloth thoroughly and lay it in the pan. Use seeds to write your initials on the damp cloth. Be sure to put the seeds on thickly. Stretch plastic wrap tightly over the pan. Cover it with newspapers to keep it dark and put it someplace warm.

When the seeds start sprouting, remove the newspaper and put the pan in a sunny window. After your initials are fully sprouted, you can eat them in a sandwich or salad!

 In the circles, number the steps in the correct order:

Name _____

All About Vanilla

 Ready:

orchid
flavor
cultivated
rootlets
pulp
aroma
extract
complicated
process
expensive
substitute
imitate
product

1. The fragrance or odor of a flower is its _____.

2. Something made from all or part of a plant is a _____ of that plant.

3. What word has the *oo* sound that you hear in the word *moon*? _____

4. This word is the opposite of cheap or inexpensive. _____

5. What is the base word found in the word imitation? _____

6. A word that rhymes with *favor* would be _____.

Set:

Vanilla is the name of a group of climbing orchids. The vanilla extract is used to flavor chocolate, all kinds of ice cream, pastry, and candy. The vanilla vine has been cultivated in Mexico for hundreds of years. Other countries also grow vanilla.

The vanilla vine has little rootlets that attach themselves to trees. The plant itself lives for about 10 years. It will produce its first crop of vanilla beans after about 3 years.

Name _____

The vanilla plant produces a fruit in the shape of a bean pod that grows to be 5 to 10 inches long. The fruit has oily black pulp that contains a large number of tiny black seeds. When the pods grow to be a yellow-black color, they are gathered and dried. While drying, the bean turns a chocolate-brown color. It will now have the flavor and aroma of vanilla as we know it.

Making the vanilla extract that you use in your home is a complicated process. The beans are chopped and boiled in alcohol and water. It is expensive to produce. Scientists have developed substitutes for real vanilla called imitation vanilla. The next time you go to the store, look for products that contain vanilla.

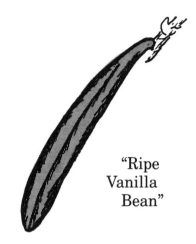

"Ripe Vanilla Bean"

Some imitation vanilla comes from the Ponderosa Pine. Its bark smells like vanilla!

 Go:

1. A word that means something has been grown is (cultivated, watered, expensive).

2. A vanilla plant will produce beans after (1,3,5) years.

3. The beans grow to be _____ to _____ inches long.

4. Inside the oily black pulp are the _____.

5. Vanilla beans are chopped and boiled to make vanilla extract. (Yes, No)

6. Name one product you like that contains vanilla. _____

7. What word in the story means a substitute for real vanilla? _____

Name _____

Handwriting—Plant Growth

soil _____

_____

minerals _____

_____

carbon dioxide _____

_____

photosynthesis _____

_____

transpiration _____

_____

nutrients _____

_____

chlorophyll _____

_____

oxygen _____

_____

energy _____

_____

water _____

_____

Name _____

Seed Distribution

As you read this story, circle the correct word in each numbered box at the bottom of this sheet.

Have you ever picked 1. _____ white, fluffy dandelion and blown on it? The wind blows the fluff and seeds away. The parachute floats in the wind and falls in a 2. _____ place. If the seed settles into the earth another dandelion may grow. Many plants 3. _____ their seeds this way.

People and animals 4. _____ on their legs. Some seeds can move, too. They have tiny hair, bristles, or hooks 5. _____ the outside edge or at one end of the seed. When it is wet, the seed swells and grips the soil. Then they 6. _____. This drying and swelling moves the seeds along.

Other seeds may be washed out by a rainstorm and carried by a stream. Plants along beaches shed their seeds onto the sand. These are carried out to 7. _____ by the tides. They 8. _____ on the water and may land on distant beaches.

Have you ever seen a cocklebur stuck to a dog's 9. _____ coat? When the dog scratches, the seeds may fall to the ground and grow. Many seeds are picked up by animals and people and "hitch-hike" to new 10. _____.

1. to a an	2. next same different	3. scatter fly bury	4. move go work	5. after in on
6. die dry float	7. sky air sea	8. float sink paddle	9. cloth jacket fur	10. houses places trees

Name _____

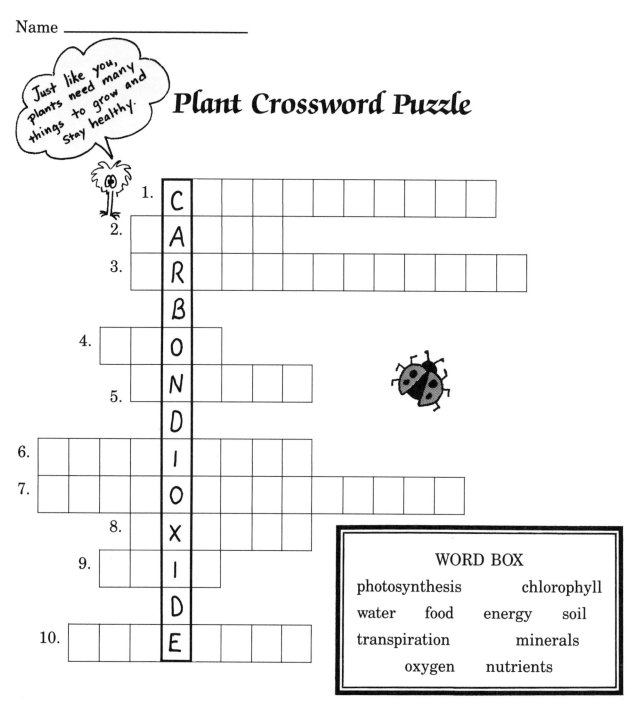

Just like you, plants need many things to grow and stay healthy.

Plant Crossword Puzzle

1. C
2. A
3. R
4. B
5. O
6. N
7. D
8. I
9. O
10. X
    I
    D
    E

WORD BOX

photosynthesis   chlorophyll

water   food   energy   soil

transpiration   minerals

oxygen   nutrients

1. the green color in most plants
2. liquid necessary for all plant and animal life
3. the evaporation of water into the air
4. nourishment that helps plants live and grow
5. the capacity to do work
6. substances that provide food and nourishment
7. how plants manufacture food
8. a gas without color, taste, or odor
9. ground, earth, or dirt
10. substances of the earth neither plant nor animal

Name _____

Photosynthesis

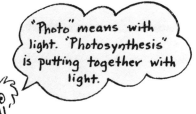

"Photo" means with light. "Photosynthesis" is putting together with light.

The stems and leaves of most plants are green. The green color is *chlorophyll*. Chlorophyll helps plants grow. It helps them make *oxygen* (O_2). Most plants take in *water* through their roots. They take in *carbon dioxide* (CO_2) through their leaves. *Heat* and *light* from the *sun* shine on the plants. This helps the chlorophyll do its job. The plant makes sugar and oxygen. The sugar helps the plant grow bigger. The oxygen goes out into the air for us to breathe. This process, called *photosynthesis*, is necessary for all plants, animals, and people to live.

 With your teacher's help, label the parts on the drawing below.

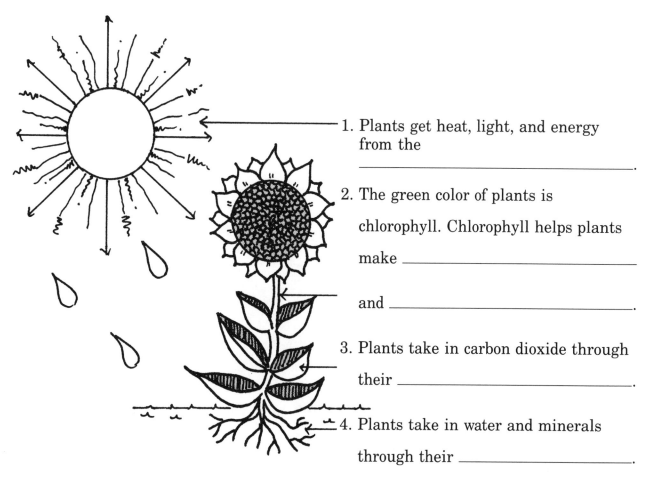

1. Plants get heat, light, and energy from the
   _____.

2. The green color of plants is chlorophyll. Chlorophyll helps plants
   make _____
   and _____.

3. Plants take in carbon dioxide through their _____.

4. Plants take in water and minerals through their _____.

Name _____

All About a Venus' Flytrap

 **Ready:**

insects digest bog nitrogen greenhouse blade lobe surface sensitive bristles fluid secrete gland capture	1. A group of small animals with 3-part bodies and 3 pairs of legs are _____. 2. An organ in the body that makes and gives out some substance is a _____. 3. The word that has the same "ew" sound as "stew" is _____. 4. This compound word is a place where plants are grown. _____ 5. What is the base word found in the word secreted? _____ 6. A word that rhymes with trade would be _____.

 Set:

The Venus' Flytrap is a "meat-eating" plant that traps insects and digests them. It grows in wet "bog" areas where the soil lacks nitrogen. The insects provide the nitrogen that the plant needs. This plant is often seen in store greenhouses.

A Venus' Flytrap plant grows to be about 1 foot high. Its leaves have 2 parts. The lower part is shaped like a blade. The upper part has 2 round "lobes" joined together. Inside the lobes are 3 or 4 sensitive hairs. The edges of the lobes have 18 sharp bristles.

Name _____

A. Fly enters.   B. Closes and traps.   C. Digests   D. Reopens and drops skeleton

If an insect touches the sensitive hairs, the lobes close. A sweet juice something like honey is secreted by glands in the lobes. The fluid helps the plant digest insects. This takes 8-10 days after which the trap opens. When the Venus' Flytrap has caught about 3 insects, the lobe withers and dies.

One interesting fact about the Venus' Flytrap is that it can tell the difference between meat and non-meat. If you put a non-meat item in the lobe, it will close. But after 24 hours it will open and drop the object out. Smart plant!

Venus was the Roman Goddess of Love!

 Go:

1. A wet, damp area is a (desert, bog, island).

2. What do insects provide for the plant? (oxygen, water, nitrogen)

3. How many feet tall will the Flytrap grow? (1, 3-4, 6-8)

4. How many parts does each leaf have? _____

5. When an insect touches the hairs, the leaves open. (Yes, No)

6. A fluid secreted by the glands helps the plant to grow. (Yes, No)

7. What word in paragraph 3 of this story means "shrinks and dries out"? _____

Name _____

A Terrarium

As you read this story, circle the correct word in each numbered box at the bottom of this sheet.

You probably know what an aquarium is. "Aqua" is a Latin word that 1. _____ "water." An aquarium is a place where fish, water snails, and water plants live in 2. _____.

"Terra" is a Latin word that means "land." A Terrarium is a glass container with soil in it where plants can be grown.

You can make a 3. _____ out of almost any kind of glass container. The bottom must be filled with soil. The soil can be higher in 4. _____ back. The surface doesn't have to be even, and it will look best if it is a bit hilly.

Small, 5. _____ plants are easiest to grow in your 6. _____. Older plants' roots will be too big. Plant your plants and place a few small rocks among them to make your terrarium look natural.

Be careful not to water your terrarium 7. _____ much. The soil should be damp, but not 8. _____. If you cover a terrarium with a pane of glass, it will stay 9. _____ for a long time between waterings and your plants will 10. _____ well.

1. says means drinks	2. sand water liquid	3. terrarium garden aquarium	4. this a the	5. green tiny young
6. terrarium house sink	7. too to two	8. dry dirty wet	9. dry damp young	10. wilt grow die

Name _____

Seed Package Math

 Use these seed packages to help you solve the problems below.

 CORN 80¢

 CARROTS 69¢

 PUMPKINS 89¢

 RADISHES 59¢

 ONIONS 75¢

1. If you bought one package each of corn seeds, pumpkin seeds, and radish seeds, how much would you spend?

    Corn costs _____.

    Pumpkins cost _____.

    Radishes cost _____.

    Together, all three cost _____.

2. If you bought one package each of pumpkins, radishes, and onions, how much would you spend?

3. If you bought one package each of corn, radishes, and onions, how much would you spend?

4. If you bought one package each of pumpkins, onions, and corn, how much would you spend?

Work Space

1.

2.

3.

4.

Bonus Box: If you bought one package of each kind of seeds, how much change would you get back from $5.00?

Watch your slant.

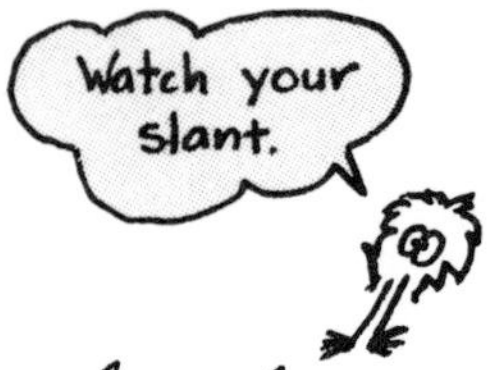

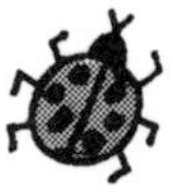

Handwriting—Plant Parts

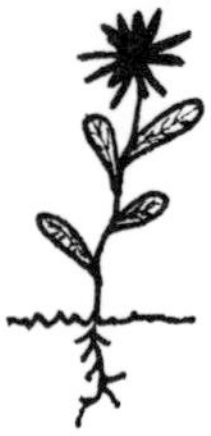

leaf _____

_____

stem _____

_____

roots _____

_____

veins _____

_____

bud _____

_____

shoot _____

_____

seedling _____

_____

sprout _____

_____

node _____

_____

root apex _____

_____

Name _____

Plant Parts

As you read this story, circle the correct word in each numbered box at the bottom of this sheet.

There are four main parts of a plant: the roots, the stem, the leaves, and the flower. Each part of the 1. _____ has a job to do.

Plant roots serve many purposes, but the most 2. _____ thing they do is soak up water and dissolved minerals from the 3. _____. The plant needs water and minerals to make food. Once the food is made, it may be stored in the roots. Roots are also 4. _____ to hold the plant firmly in the ground.

The stems of a plant are 5. _____ tiny bundles of thin pipes. They carry water and minerals from the roots to the leaves. They also 6. _____ food to all other parts.

Green leaves are important 7. _____ they make food needed by the plant. The food is sugar. All that a green plant 8. _____ to make sugar is sunlight, air, and water.

Part of a plant's flower becomes the fruit, which contains the seeds. Each seed contains a 9. _____ plant and food that it can use to grow 10. _____ enough to have its own roots and green leaves.

1. plant garden seed	2. funny important strange	3. soil air sky	4. big furry needed	5. really many like
6. leave make carry	7. because but and	8. likes needs thinks	9. baby green huge	10. fat lazy big

Name _____

All About Aloe-Vera

 Ready:

| juice |
| height |
| rosette |
| stalk |
| red |
| fibers |
| coarse |
| bitter |
| evaporate |
| cultures |
| jagged |
| dye |

1. The main stem of a plant is its _____.

2. Something with a notched or crooked edge could be called_____.

3. What word has the ō sound that you hear in *toes*? _____

4. _____ is the opposite of sweet or mild.

5. What word means to remove water from something? _____

6. What base word is found in the word reddish? _____

 Set:

Aloe is a plant that grows in warm countries. Aloe plants range in height from a few inches to 30 feet or more. The leaves of many aloe plants become very large. They are long and sharply pointed at the ends. The outside edges are jagged and have hooks on them. These leaves usually grow directly out of the ground, not on a stem. The leaves form what is called a rosette. From the center of this rosette, the flowering stalk grows. The flower of the aloe plant is usually yellow or reddish and shaped like a tube.

Name _____

Some kinds of aloe plants have fibers in their leaves that are used for making rope, fishing nets, and coarse cloth. Other aloe plants have finer fibers that are used to make lace, and some are used to make violet-colored dye.

The leaves of some aloe plants have a clear bitter juice or liquid in them. This liquid is dried by evaporation and then used in medicines. If you should happen to have a minor burn, you can cut a piece of leaf from the aloe plant and squeeze the juice onto your burned skin. This soothing liquid will ease the pain. Many native cultures used aloe plants to treat illnesses and injuries. Many creams and lotions that you see in stores contain some form of aloe.

In New Mexico you can buy Aloe-flavored, frozen yogurt!

 Go:

1. The aloe plant grows in _____ _____.

2. The leaves grow directly from the ground and form a _____.

3. The tube-like flowers are _____ or _____.

4. What color dye is made from aloe fibers? _____

5. The clear aloe juice tastes _____.

6. Aloe juice on a burn can help ease the _____.

7. What word in the last paragraph means to dry or remove moisture from the plant?

_____

Name _____

More About Plant Parts

 There are four main parts of a plant. They are the *roots, leaves, stem,* and *flower*. Use a dictionary to help you write a definition for each part.

1. roots _____

_____

2. stem _____

_____

3. leaves _____

_____

4. flowers _____

_____

On the drawing below label the main parts of a plant:

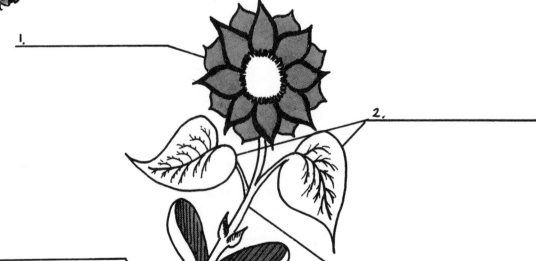

Name _____

Flowers Word Search

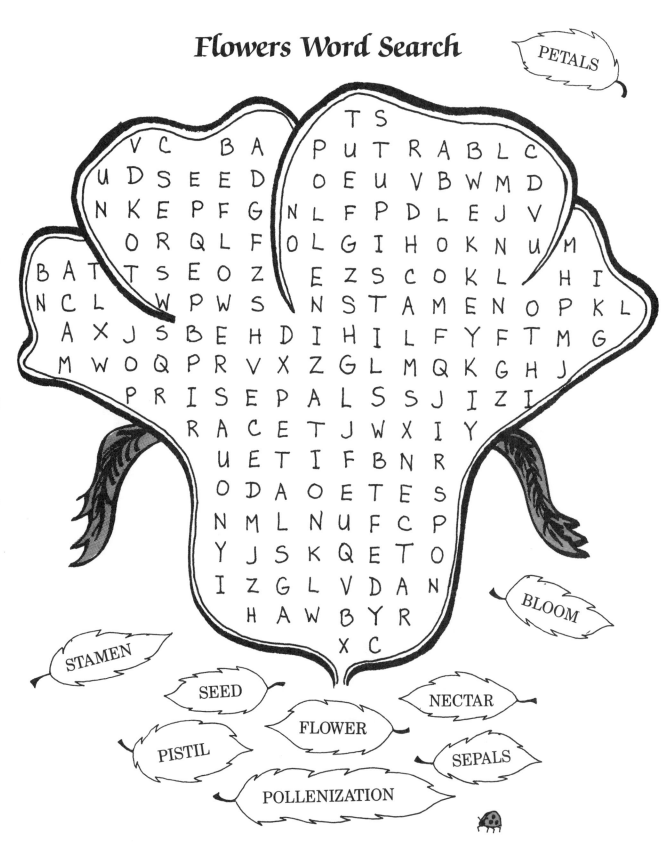

PETALS

```
            T S
    V C   B A   P U T R A B L C
  U D S E E D   O E U V B W M D
  N K E P F G   N L F P D L E J V
    O R Q L F   O L G I H O K N U   M
B A T T S E O Z   E Z S C O K L   H I
N C L   W P W S   N S T A M E N   O P K L
A X J   S B E H D I H I L F Y F T M G
M W O Q P R V X Z G L M Q K G H J
  P R I S E P A L S S J I Z I
  R A C E T J W X I Y
  U E T I F B N R
  O D A O E T E S
  N M L N U F C P
  Y J S K Q E T O
  I Z G L V D A N
  H A W B Y R
        X C
```

STAMEN

SEED

PISTIL

FLOWER

POLLENIZATION

NECTAR

SEPALS

BLOOM

Name _____

Flower Parts

There are four main parts of a flower. They are the *sepals*, *petals*, *stamens*, and *pistil*. Use a dictionary to help you write definitions for the parts.

1. sepal _____

_____

2. petal _____

_____

3. stamen _____

_____

4. pistil _____

_____

Label the four main parts on the flower below. With your teacher's help, also label the *seed, ovary, pollen tube, pollen stigma,* and *anther.*

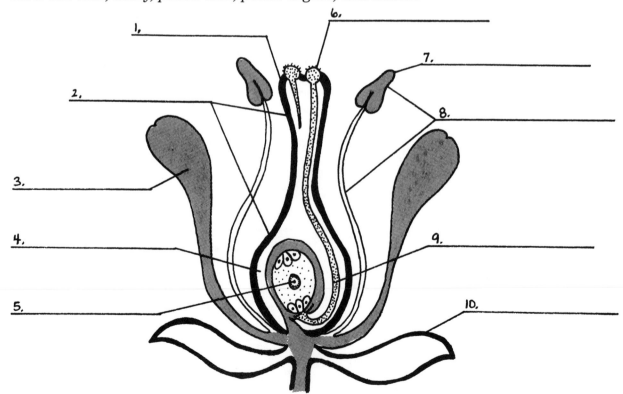

Name _____

The Flower

As you read this story, circle the correct word in each numbered box at the bottom of this sheet.

The flowers of plants and trees bloom almost

everywhere on 1. _____. Some flowers grow on

high mountains. 2. _____ live in shallow parts of the ocean. Even hot, dry deserts have many bright blossoms.

Flowers are the reproductive parts of plants.

The plants 3. _____ not develop seeds and reproduce without them. We all depend on flowering plants for our food.

A typical 4. _____ has four flower parts attached to its stalk. The sepals, which are usually green and tough, protect the flower bud. The petals

are usually delicate and have some 5. _____ other than green. The petals are often sweet smelling to attract insects. The stamens have a slender stalk with pollen sacs at their tips. The pistil contains the ovary where the plant's seeds develop.

When the flower 6. _____ the pollen grains are carried from the stamen of one

flower to the pistil of 7. _____ flower. Pollen is carried by wind or insects. The

8. _____ grain develops a 9. _____ tube that grows down the pistil into the ovary.

Here a 10. _____ will be produced.

1. Mars Earth Venus	2. Others This None	3. could couldn't won't	4. tree stick plant	5. size color scent
6. closes dies opens	7. insects another some	8. wind pollen sand	9. huge tiny closed	10. seed root flower

Name _____

All About the Artichoke

 **Ready:**

| artichoke |
| vegetable |
| thistle |
| Jerusalem |
| artichoke |
| divided |
| edible |
| prickly |
| marinated |
| related |
| sunflower |

1. Something with many stickers could be called _____.

2. _____ means fit to eat.

3. What word means "in the same family"? _____

4. What word means the opposite of multiplied? _____

5. What word rhymes with whistle? _____

6. What word is a compound word? _____

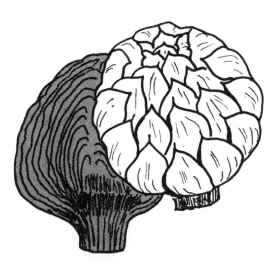

 Set:

The artichoke plant has a flower bud that you may have eaten as a vegetable for your dinner.

The globe artichoke is a large gray-green plant that looks like a thistle. You can grow these plants from seeds, but usually artichokes are divided to make new plants. The artichoke plant lives for 3 to 4 years and grows to 2 to 3 feet high. It has large prickly leaves. The flower buds of the globe artichoke may be eaten. They are grown in California and are transported all over the United States.

To eat an artichoke, you must first steam cook the bud to soften it. Not all of the bud can be eaten. There are thistle-like parts in the middle that you cannot eat, but you can eat the soft part of the leaves and the base of the bud. Many people like to eat artichoke leaves hot and dip them in melted butter. Other people like to eat the artichoke cold. They chill it and then dip the leaves in mayonnaise. Marinated artichoke hearts are soaked in oil and spices. Then they are served with salads.

There are many other types of artichoke plants. The Jerusalem artichoke is related to the sunflower. It grows to be 5 to 12 feet tall and has yellow flowers that bloom in the fall. The tubers or roots are edible. The Jerusalem artichoke grows wild in some parts of the United States.

 Go:

1. The part of the artichoke we eat is the _____ _____.

2. The globe artichoke grows to be _____ to _____ feet tall.

3. Can an artichoke be grown from seeds? (Yes, No, Doesn't Say)

4. The Jerusalem artichoke is related to the _____.

5. If a plant can be eaten, it is _____.

6. Artichokes that have been soaked in oil and spices are _____ artichokes.

7. What word in paragraph 2 of this story means "moved from one place to another"?

Name _____

All About Chewing Gum

 **Ready:**

sapodilla
chicle
slitting
collecting
pure
purified
filters
liquid
peppermint
spearmint
flavoring
ingredients
rubber

1. Gathering or bringing together is the same as _____.

2. _____ means cleaned or made pure.

3. What word has the same *u* sound that you hear in the word *cup*? _____

4. Bubble gum is made elastic by adding other _____.

5. What base word is found in the word purified? _____

6. The gum base from the sapodilla tree is called _____.

 Set:

Long ago Greek people chewed a form of chewing gum. A thousand years ago, the Mayan people of Yucatán chewed gum. Gum was brought to the United States in the 1860s, about 120 years ago.

Name _____

The "chew" in chewing gum comes from the sapodilla tree. Workmen remove the gum base called chicle by slitting the bark of the trees. The white, milky chicle flows out into buckets placed at the bottom of the trees. It is collected and boiled in large pots. The chicle is then formed into blocks and sent to a factory.

In the factory, the chicle is purified and cleaned by filters. Then the purified chicle is mixed with flavorings like peppermint or spearmint in large kettles. The flavored gum is rolled into a thin sheet and cut into pieces by automatic machines.

Candy-coated gums are coated in whirling copper pans. Bubble gum begins just like regular gum. Later it is made firm and elastic by adding other ingredients including rubber. Bubble gum must be more elastic so that you can blow bubbles with it.

Gum is packaged and sealed by machines. Then it is loaded in trucks and delivered to stores for us to buy.

 Go:

1. Chicle comes from a tree called _____.

2. _____ is the milky white liquid that flows from the tree.

3. Two flavorings used in gum are _____ and _____.

4. What cuts the gum into pieces? _____

5. When was gum introduced to the United States? _____

6. What is one ingredient added to gum to make it elastic so we can blow bubbles? __

_____

7. What word in the fourth paragraph means to turn around and around? _____

Name _____

Plant Products

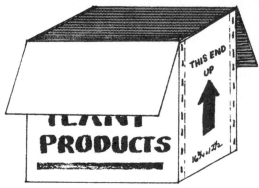

As you read this story, circle the correct word in each numbered box at the bottom of this sheet.

The world is filled with over 350,000 different kinds of plants. Without plants, there would not be life as we know it. Animals could not live without plants for food.

Plants are the source of thousands of products that we use 1. _____ day. The most

familiar plant products are 2. _____ .

Plants are the source of cotton, linen, and many other fibers that are 3. _____ into cloth or made into twine or rope.

Plants give us shelter. Lumber for the construction of homes and buildings comes

from 4. _____ . The paper on which you are reading and the pencil with which you write also come from trees.

Rubber is made from latex, which comes from 5. _____ trees. Other forms of rubber are made into golf balls, car tires, dental fillings, and chewing gum.

Plants are used to tan animal skins when they are made into 6. _____ . Some

dyes comes 7. _____ plants and are used to dye cloth many 8. _____ . The sticky

liquid from evergreen trees is used to 9. _____ turpentine, varnish, and printers' ink.

Medicines come from herbs and other 10. _____ , too. As you can see, we use plant products in many ways every day.

© 1987 by The Center for Applied Research in Education, Inc.

1. have use every	2. leaves foods bricks	3. woven sewed thread	4. trees bushes twigs	5. big old rubber
6. food leather coats	7. to of from	8. kinds colors sizes	9. make boil grow	10. animals minerals plants

Name _____

More About Plant Products

   Most of our food comes from plants. Animals eat plants, so we use plants even when we eat steak or drink milk. We also eat the seeds, roots, stems, leaves, and fruits of many plants.
   Below, list foods you eat that are seeds, roots, stems, leaves, and fruits. By the cow, list food we get from plant-eating animals.

Seeds

_____
_____
_____
_____
_____

Roots

_____
_____
_____
_____
_____

Stems

_____
_____
_____
_____
_____

Leaves

_____
_____
_____
_____

Fruits

_____
_____
_____
_____

Others

_____
_____
_____
_____

Bee's Specialty

© 1987 by The Center for Applied Research in Education, Inc.

WORD BOX					
garden	pistil	petals	stamen	blossom	roses
flower	bloom	seed	sepals	nectar	rain

1. A flower of a fruit tree is sometimes called a

   _____.

2. _____ are red. Violets are blue.
3. The pistil and stamen are parts of a

   _____.

4. _____ is a sweet juice.

5. _____ is a moisture from clouds that makes flowers grow.

6. The colorful _____ of a flower attract insects.

7. Green _____ protect the bud of the flower.

8. If you plant a _____, a new plant may grow.

9. The _____ is the flower part that produces pollen.

10. The enlarged base of the flower that produces seeds is the _____.

11. Most flowers and blossoms _____ or open in spring.

12. Flowers and vegetables grow in a _____.

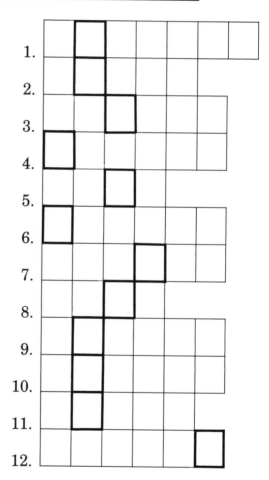

The clue for the following word is: bee's specialty.

6	2	1	11	8	4	5	Z	7	9	10	3	12

Name _____

Plant Graph

Some children grew corn plants for their class project. They started a graph to show how tall each plant had grown. Candy's plant was 6 inches tall. Above her name, she colored one square for each inch her plant had grown. Finish the graph by coloring the correct number of squares for each child's plant. Then use the graph to help you answer the questions.

* Ray's plant was 4 inches tall.
* Glenn's plant was 6 inches tall.
* Randi's plant was 7 inches tall.
* Shawn's plant was 5 inches tall.

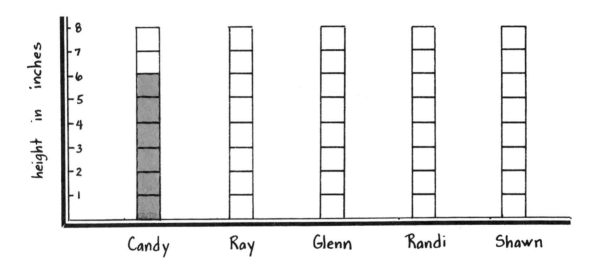

1. Whose plant grew tallest? _____

2. Who had the shortest plant? _____

3. Name the two children whose plants were the same size. _____

4. How much taller was Glenn's plant than Ray's? _____

5. How many plants were taller than Shawn's? _____

6. How much shorter was Shawn's plant than Candy's? _____

Name _____

Plants Quick Check

 Use the word box to help you complete the sentences

pistil	photosynthesis	flowers	roots	pollen
chlorophyll	petals	seed	water	powder

1. The _____ of a plant germinates to start a new plant.

2. _____ is the process plants use to make food.

3. The _____ are the reproductive parts of the plant.

4. _____ is the liquid necessary for all life.

5. The green color in most plants that helps produce sugar is _____.

Write "Yes" for true, and write "No" for not true.

6. _____ The tiny plant within a seed is an embryo.

7. _____ Cotyledons are a plant's first leaves.

8. _____ Animals get most of their food from plants.

9. _____ The node is the main part of a plant.

10. _____ Leaves are sweet-smelling to attract insects.

11. _____ We eat the root of the carrot plant.

12. _____ Chewing gum comes from plants.

★ _____

★ _____

★ _____

What things do you like that come from plants?

Name _____

Handwriting—Insects

Sloppy handwriting really "bugs" me!

antennae _____

_____

thorax _____

_____

abdomen _____

_____

spider _____

_____

pupa _____

_____

cocoon _____

_____

caterpillar _____

_____

molt _____

_____

adult _____

_____

insect _____

_____

Name _____

 # Insect Characteristics

Insects are found nearly everywhere on the earth. There are far more insects than people or any other animal. Some insects are beautiful. Some are scary. Some insects buzz and fly. Some hop and chirp. Some insects crawl and creep, while others hardly move at all. Some insects are helpful and others can hurt us. Insects can be any color of the rainbow. All insects are interesting to study.

One way that you can identify an insect is to count its legs. All adult insects have 6 legs. An insect uses its legs 3 at a time. It moves the front and back legs on one side with the middle leg on the opposite side.

Most insects have either 2 or 4 wings. They do not flap their wings like birds do. Insects move their wings in a motion shaped like a figure eight.

Another way to study insects is by looking at the parts of their bodies. Insects' bodies are divided into 3 main parts:

*The *head* had the mouth, eyes, and antennae.
*The *thorax* or middle body holds the muscles, wings, and legs.
*The *abdomen* contains organs for digesting food and reproduction as well as the heart.

Use a dictionary to help you write definitions for the words below:

1. insect _____

_____

2. antennae _____

_____

3. adult _____

_____

4. head _____

_____

5. thorax _____

_____

6. abdomen _____

_____

Name ───────

An Insect's Body

  Label the head, thorax, abdomen, antennae, leg, wing, and mouth on the drawing below.

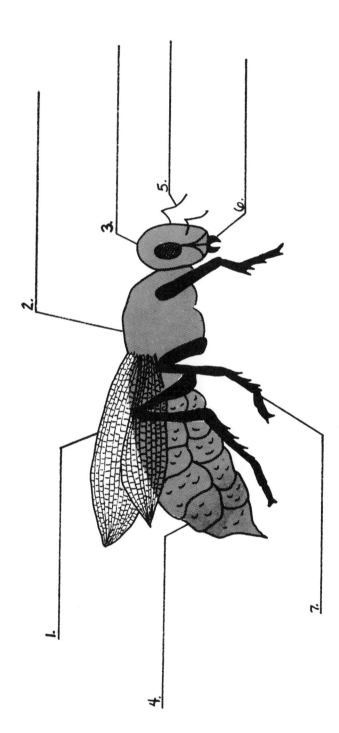

1.

2.

3.

4.

5.

6.

7.

Name _____

All About Spiders

 Ready:

antennae
molt
skeleton
prey
snare
spinnerets
abdomen
tarantula
cocoon
survive

1. The word that has the same "oo" sound as "soon" is _____.

2. The spinning organs on the spider's abdomen are called

 _____.

3. _____ is another word that means the same as "trap."

4. A word that rhymes with "day" is _____.

5. The word that has the same "i" sound as "five" is _____.

 Set:

Spiders are *not* insects! They are different from insects in many ways. A spider has 8 legs instead of 6. The spider's body has only 2 main parts and they never have wings. Spiders also have no jaws or antennae as insects do.

There are more than 50,000 kinds of spiders. Some are tiny. Some are as large as your hand. Few spiders are harmful. Most are helpful because they eat insects.

Spiders have no bones. Their hard outer body is their skeleton. As they grow, spiders molt or shed this skeleton and grow a new one in a larger size.

Spiders get their food by either hunting or trapping insects. The hunting spiders chase their prey or wait and attack insects passing nearby. Many spiders build webs to snare their food.

 The web is made of silk thread from the spinnerets under the spider's abdomen. Each kind of spider has its own web pattern. A single web may take several days to complete.

The spider kills by stinging with its poisonous fangs. Then the prey is wrapped in silk thread. The spiders eat by sucking the fluid from the insect. A spider can live for almost a year on food stored in its abdomen.

Many types of spiders live for only one year, but the large tarantula can live up to 20 years. Spiders lay eggs in a silk sac or cocoon. While the baby spiders are in the cocoon, they eat each other! Only the strongest baby spiders survive.

Go:

1. A spider has (2, 3, 4) body parts.
2. _____ are not insects!
3. While they are inside the cocoon, baby spiders will eat each other. (Yes, No)
4. Liquid silk comes from the spider's _____.
5. Most spiders are quite small, but some grow as large as your _____.
6. A tarantula is a large spider that can live up to (3, 10, 20) years.
7. Spiders lay eggs in a silk sac or _____.
8. The word from paragraph 3 in this story that means "to shed" is _____.

Name _____

The Monarch

As you read this story, circle the correct word in each numbered box at the bottom of this sheet.

Did you know that a Monarch butterfly is like a skunk? Like the skunk, the Monarch produces an odor to protect itself. A scent pouch 1. _____ a strong smell that birds know will 2. _____ bad.

The Monarch 3. _____ is also similar to a bird. Like a bird, the Monarch migrates. It travels to warm places in the South when fall comes. They 4. _____ North in the spring.

The Monarch doesn't start out as a butterfly. It begins life as an egg attached to a milkweed plant. The 5. _____ egg hatches out a caterpillar or larvae. The caterpillar spends its time eating, 6. _____, and shedding its skin. When it molts for the last time, it even sheds its legs!

The caterpillar attaches itself to a 7. _____ or leaf and forms a shell. This shell hardens into a pupa. 8. _____ the changing or metamorphosis is happening inside the pupa. When the pupa finally splits 9. _____, a Monarch butterfly comes out. Its orange and black wings are crumpled and damp. Soon they will 10. _____ in the sun and the new Monarch will be able to fly.

1. loses produces likes	2. taste look feel	3. insect butterfly cocoon	4. leave return gone	5. huge bird tiny
6. dying thinking growing	7. twig dog car	8. Not Now Know	9. closed open back	10. fall wet dry

Name _____

An Ant House

An ant colony is like a miniature house. Female workers build many rooms joined by pathways or tunnels. In her own special room, the queen lays her eggs. Workers move the eggs to the hatching room. Later the larvae are moved to a nursery. Other rooms are used for storing food. There is even a "trash" room the ants use as a combination garbage dump and cemetery!

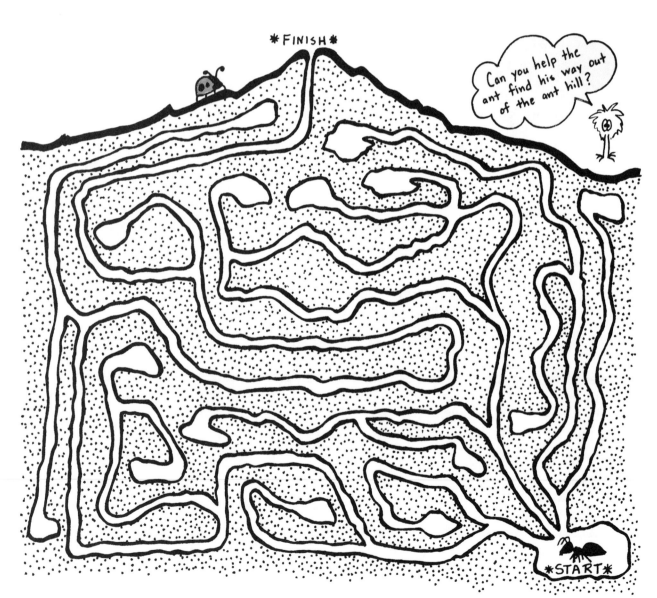

Name _____

What's a Bird?

Many people think that "flying" makes a bird. That is not always true. Neither ostriches nor penguins fly. Bats and flying fish can fly, but they are not birds. The one sure way to recognize a bird is by its feathers. Only birds have feathers.

All birds have feathers. This makes them different from all other animals. Birds have three kinds of feathers. The contour feathers give the bird its shape and color. Flight feathers help the bird to fly and down feathers keep it warm. You may have seen warm coats or comforters filled with down feathers. Birds molt or shed their feathers at least once a year. There may be as many as 11,000 feathers on a mallard duck!

Something else a bird has that other creatures do not is a gizzard. The gizzard is an organ with strong muscles that helps the bird digest food. Birds have no teeth. Their gizzards "chew" their food by grinding it between pebbles that the birds have swallowed.

All birds hatch from eggs. Birds are many shapes, sizes, and colors, but their bodies are all very much alike. Birds have strong, thin bones. Some of their bones are hollow to make the bird light enough to fly. Birds can see and hear well, but have poor senses of taste and smell. Just like you, birds are warm-blooded. This means that their body temperature is always about the same, even in very warm or very cold weather.

Small birds, such as the hummingbirds or wrens, usually live about 1 or 2 years. Larger birds, such as eagles or geese, often live 15 to 20 years. Parrots live longer than most other birds. Some have been known to live more than 60 years!

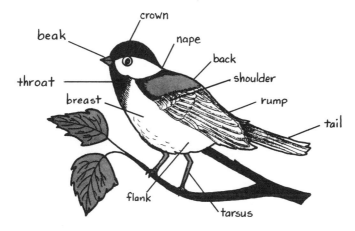

Write "Yes" in front of the true statements. Write "No" in front of the false statements.

1. _____ Birds have strong, heavy bones.
2. _____ All birds have feathers.
3. _____ Some creatures that are not birds can fly.
4. _____ All birds hatch from eggs.
5. _____ Birds never live more than 20 years.
6. _____ Bats and flying fish are types of birds.
7. _____ Birds are warm-blooded.
8. _____ All birds have teeth.
9. _____ A gizzard is a kind of small reptile.
10. _____ Birds have three different kinds of feathers.

Name _____

Eggs, Eggs, Eggs

As you read this story, circle the correct word in each numbered box at the bottom of this sheet.

An egg has four parts. The 1. _____ part is the yolk. The clear or white part 2. _____ the yolk is the albumen. The egg is protected by a thin, rubbery membrane and a 3. _____ shell.

Like all birds, chickens hatch from eggs. The chick grows 4. _____ the egg for three weeks. The egg white or albumen and the yoke are food for the growing 5. _____. Mother hens sit on the eggs to keep them warm. 6. _____ few hours she must turn the eggs. If she did not the chicks would stick to the inside of their egg shells.

After 21 7. _____ the chick will begin to hatch. First the chick pecks a 8. _____ hole in the shell with its "egg tooth." This is a small, hard knob at the end of its beak. It takes about six 9. _____ for the chick to free itself. The baby chick pecks for awhile and then rests. When it finally wiggles free of the shell, the chick is tired and wet. In about 2 hours the new chick's downy 10. _____ will be fluffy and dry.

1. yellow green black	2. from inside around	3. hard clear broken	4. outside inside under	5. hen chick egg
6. Never Many Every	7. days weeks months	8. huge black small	9. hours months years	10. hairs feathers feet

Name _____

Beaks and Feet

The beaks and feet of birds are well adapted to different environments. Match each picture with its description.

1. _____ A "grasping foot" has strong, curved claws for catching and carrying prey.

2. _____ The "cracker beak" is short and strong for cracking hard-shelled seeds.

3. _____ A "climbing foot" with sharp claws has two forward toes and two backward toes.

4. _____ The sharp, hard "chisel beak" cuts holes in trees and digs out insects.

5. _____ A "perching foot" has three slender forward toes and one slender backward toe for balance.

6. _____ The long, sharp "spear beak" is for catching fish and water animals.

7. _____ A "swimming foot" has skin between its three toes for paddling in the water.

8. _____ The "prober beak" plucks insects from plants much like a pair of tweezers.

9. _____ A large "wading foot" has three forward toes with no webbing between them.

Name _____

All About the Emperor

 **Ready:**

| marine |
| waterproof |
| blubber |
| rookeries |
| territory |
| belly |
| waddles |
| huddles |
| crèche |
| protect |

1. Another word that means the same as "abdomen" is _____.

2. _____ is a compound word.

3. The base word in "protection" is _____.

4. _____ means "having to do with salt water."

5. The word with the same "oo" sound as "book" is _____.

6. Another word for "fat" is _____.

 Set:

The Emperor Penguin is an unusual marine bird. It is called a flightless bird because it cannot fly. Its wings have no quills. Over many millions of years the penguin's wings have changed into flippers. Its flippers make the **Emperor** an excellent swimmer and diver.

An adult Emperor Penguin is about 4 feet tall and weighs about 75 pounds. They live in Antarctica and spend much of their time in the water eating fish. Their short feathers are waterproof and they have thick layers of fat to protect them from the cold.

Name _____

Emperor Penguins live in colonies called "rookeries." Thousands of penguins may live in one rookery, but each pair has its own nesting territory. The female Emperor lays one egg on the ice and then returns to the sea. The male penguin keeps the egg warm until it hatches. He rolls the egg up onto the top of his feet and covers it with his belly. He waddles around with the egg on his feet and huddles together with other males to keep warm. While caring for the egg, the male Emperor Penguin does not eat.

In two months the baby Emperor Penguin hatches, and the female penguin returns. She cares for the new chick while the male goes out to sea to hunt for food. Both the mother and father care for the young penguin. The chicks are kept all together in groups called crèches for warmth and protection. The babies snuggle together in the center of the crèche. The adults gather around them to keep them warm and safe. The young Emperor Penguins stay with their parents for about 6 months. Then they are ready to be on their own.

Crèche means "nursery" in French.

 Go:

1. A colony of penguins is called a _____.

2. An Emperor Penguin adult can weigh about 75 pounds and be (3, 4, 5) feet tall.

3. While waiting for the eggs to hatch, the male penguin doesn't eat. (Yes, No)

4. Another word for the nursery where the baby penguins are kept warm is a _____.

5. Baby penguins can leave their parents and take care of themselves when they are

   _____ months old.

6. The female penguin lays two eggs on the ice. (Yes, No)

Name _____

Miranda's Eggs

Miranda's family has 36 chickens. For a week Miranda kept track of how many eggs the chickens laid. Use her chart to help solve the problems.

EGG CHART

Sunday . . . . 26 eggs

Monday . . . . 29 eggs

Tuesday . . . . 25 eggs

Wednesday . . . . . 17 eggs

Thursday . . . . . . 30 eggs

Friday . . . . 22 eggs

Saturday . . . . 20 eggs

1. How many eggs did the chickens lay on Sunday and Monday?

    They laid ____ eggs Sunday.

    They laid ____ eggs Monday.

    They laid ____ eggs in two days.

2. How many eggs did the chickens lay on Tuesday and Wednesday?

3. How many eggs did the chickens lay on Thursday, Friday, and Saturday?

4. How many eggs did the chickens lay on Sunday, Monday, and Tuesday?

work space

1.

2.

3.

4.

Bonus Box: How many eggs did Miranda's chickens lay in all seven days? If they laid the same number of eggs each week, how many eggs would they lay in 5 weeks?

Sea Turtles

As you read this story, circle the correct word in each numbered box at the bottom of this sheet.

The adult Green Sea Turtle can be more than 4 feet long and weigh 300 pounds. Many of 1. _____ turtles live in the tropical waters near Brazil. To mate and lay their eggs, they 2. _____ 2000 miles to Ascension Island in the South Atlantic.

The female turtle drags herself ashore with her flattened 3. _____. It is hard work to pull her huge body up the sandy beach. Finally the 4. _____ turtle sniffs her way beyond the high tide line. Here she hollows out a shallow pit for her body. Then, with her back flippers she digs a hole about 2 feet 5. _____. Into this hole she lays her eggs. They look like white ping-pong 6. _____. The turtle may lay 100 leathery eggs before covering her nest. Then she returns to the 7. _____.

The sun warms the sand and nest below. In 2 months the eggs hatch. Then the 8. _____ turtles begin the dangerous trip down the 9. _____ to the sea. Birds feast on the baby turtles. In the 10. _____, fish wait for their share of the meal. From the 100 eggs, only a few young turtles will survive.

A mother sea turtle lays eggs only once every 2 or 3 years.

1. them	2. fly	3. shell	4. lazy	5. deep
these	walk	flippers	small	beside
other	swim	head	tired	high
6. balls	7. city	8. baby	9. grass	10. air
paddles	grasses	old	water	water
nets	ocean	adult	beach	sand

Name _____

These creatures hibernate to protect themselves from cold temperatures.

Reptiles and Amphibians

Reptiles and amphibians belong to a large group of animals with backbones. All of these animals are called vertebrates.

There are four groups of reptiles. They are snakes, crocodilians, lizards, and turtles. All reptiles are cold-blooded. Their bodies stay the same temperature as their surroundings. They have lungs and breathe air. Most have tough, scaly skin that is dry and never slimy. All reptiles begin life on land. Most hatch from eggs. Some are born alive because the eggs hatch inside the mother. Dinosaurs are extinct reptiles. Compare them with living reptiles and you will see that they are alike in many ways.

There are four groups of amphibians. They are frogs, toads, newts, and salamanders. Amphibians are cold-blooded. They have lungs, but they are not as well adapted as the reptile's lungs. Amphibians are not well adapted to life on land. They breathe through their skin, which must be kept moist. Amphibians lay their eggs in water. When they are young they look like fish and breathe with gills. As adults they breathe with lungs and live part of the time on land. The word "amphibian" means "living in two places."

Read each sentence. If the sentence is true about reptiles write "R" on the line. If it is true about amphibians write "A." If it is true about both groups write both letters.

1. _____ They lay their eggs in the water.
2. _____ Crocodilians belong to this group of animals.
3. _____ Their tough, scaly skin is dry and never slimy.
4. _____ They are cold-blooded.
5. _____ They breathe with lungs.
6. _____ Their name means "living in two places."
7. _____ They have skin that must be kept moist.
8. _____ They belong to a large group of animals with backbones called vertebrates.

Name _____

Which Is It?

 Look at the pictures below. Under the name of each animal, write "reptile" if it is a reptile. Write "amphibian" if it is an amphibian.

salamander _____

frog _____

turtle _____

snake _____

lizard _____

Name _____

All About Alligators and Crocodiles

 Ready:

shallow
cigar-shaped
powerful
submerged
heavy
clutch
incubator
survive
snout
blunt

1. The base word in "heavier" is _____.

2. _____ means "to be under the surface of the water."

3. A word with the same "ou" sound as in "out" is _____.

4. If something is shaped like a long oval, it is _____.

5. A word that means "rounded off or not pointed" is _____.

6. Something full of strength is _____.

 Set:

Alligators and crocodiles are members of the largest living group of reptiles. They live in the shallow waters of tropical regions. Alligators and crocodiles have cigar-shaped bodies. Both have short strong legs for walking and powerful tails for swimming. Both have eyes and nostrils that stick up from their faces. This allows them to see and breathe while mostly submerged.

Alligators and crocodiles lay eggs on land. The female builds a nest about 7 feet wide out of rotting plants and leaves. Here she lays up to 50 white, hard-shelled eggs.

Name _____

The clutch or group of eggs stays covered in the nest for 2 to 3 months. The rotting plants of the nest keep the eggs warm like an incubator. When the eggs hatch, the mother digs the babies out of the nest.

Baby alligators and crocodiles are about 8 inches long. They will grow about 12 inches a year for several years. Adults are usually 7 to 12 feet long.

Alligators and crocodiles are very much alike, but there are differences. Alligators are heavier than crocodiles. For this reason crocodiles are quicker and more active. Both have long mouths called snouts. A crocodile's snout is pointed. An alligator's snout is shorter and more blunt.

Adult alligators and crocodiles have 50 to 80 sharp teeth. The 4th tooth is much larger than the other teeth. You can tell an alligator from a crocodile by whether or not you see teeth when its mouth is shut. When a crocodile's mouth is closed you can see the larger 4th tooth. An alligator's 4th tooth fits into a pocket in the jaw. It can't be seen when the mouth is closed.

The Crocodile Bird eats insects living on the crocodile!

 Go:

1. Alligators and crocodiles are reptiles. (Yes, No)

2. Both use their powerful _____ for swimming.

3. Alligators and crocodiles have long mouths called _____.

4. Can you see an alligator's teeth when its mouth is closed? _____

5. What 2 things stick up above the water that allow these animals to breathe and see?

_____, _____

6. Is the 4th tooth larger, smaller, or the same as the other teeth in these animals?

_____

Name _____

All About Snakes

 **Ready:**

reptiles temperature environment scales backbone grip prey vibrations digest mammals

1. Your _____ is the area you live in and the things around you.

2. A homonym for "pray" is _____.

3. _____ is a compound word.

4. A word that means "how hot or cold something is" would be _.

_____

5. A word that rhymes with "trip" is _____.

6. Lizards, snakes, and turtles are all types of _____.

 Set:

Snakes are reptiles with no legs. Like all reptiles, they are cold-blooded. This means that the snake's temperature goes up and down with the temperature of its environment.

There are more than 2,400 kinds of snakes. They are all sizes and many colors. The smallest snakes are less than 5 inches long. The largest snake, the Python, can grow to more than 30 feet in length. That is about as long as a classroom!

Most snakes move by bending from side to side. The backbone of a snake has about 300 bones. All those bones help the snake to bend, crawl, and climb. The snake's scales also help it to move. Snakes grip the ground with the scales on their stomachs. Snakes rid themselves of worn scales by shedding or molting the outer layer of their skin.

Name _____

Snakes usually hatch from eggs. A few, like the Garter Snake, are born alive like mammals. A mother Garter Snake may give birth to 50 snakes at a time. This sounds like a lot, but the Python often lays 100 eggs at one time!

A snake's fangs are sharp, but they are not made for chewing. Snakes swallow their food whole. They capture prey by injecting venom or by coiling and crushing. After the prey is swallowed it moves to the stomach. Here strong juices digest everything but hair and feathers!

Snakes touch and smell with their long, forked tongue. Snakes cannot hear sounds through the air. They can only feel vibrations on the ground. People once thought snakes could be charmed by flute music. Snakes may sway with the flute player, but they can't hear the music.

Snakes' eyes are always open. I wonder how you know if they are asleep!?

 Go:

1. Snakes usually hatch from _____.

2. Snakes use their _____to touch and smell.

3. The backbone of a snake has about (30, 300, 3,000) bones.

4. A snake's fangs are for chewing. (Yes, No)

5. The largest snake, a Python, can grow to be as long as an average classroom.

   (Yes, No)

6. Snakes feel vibrations on the ground but they can't _____ sounds in the air.

Name _____

A Fishy Word Search

Look for each of these words in the word search. The words can be found either across or down.

SCALES
SWIM BLADDER
FRESH WATER
SEAHORSE

EGGS
SALMON

SPAWN
SWIMMING
SALT WATER
COLD BLOODED

GILLS
FINS

```
A B K R D E N M C L C
S P F S W I M M I N G O
E W Q R C P O E G G S M L
U A I U E T G S F A K A L D
I X D M K S P A W N T R L V B
E E F B Y H O J G F U V M U L
V G S A L T W A T E R Q N O X O B
U H I D I B A Z A H J I H A U N Z O L
S C A L E S D O T I O I Q E R Y S D K
S X T F J C D V E S E A H O R S E E Y
  Y U A E Z R G I P O F M F W D G
  R E A E H U G I L L S J Z
  I O W J K N A C D P
  D M X L Q S E B O A
  U N S R   N I C
  O T   A H B
```

© 1987 by The Center for Applied Research in Education, Inc.

Name _____

Seahorses

Most fish lay eggs in the water. Seahorses are fish, but they do something quite different with their eggs. The mother seahorse lays her eggs in a special pouch on the father seahorse's abdomen. Here he safely carries the eggs while they develop. In about 45 days the eggs hatch. Then the father bends and squirms to push the baby seahorses out into the water. He may have 200 babies. Once they are free of the pouch, the young seahorses can care for themselves. The father's job is done.

Help the baby seahorses find a way out of the seaweed maze.

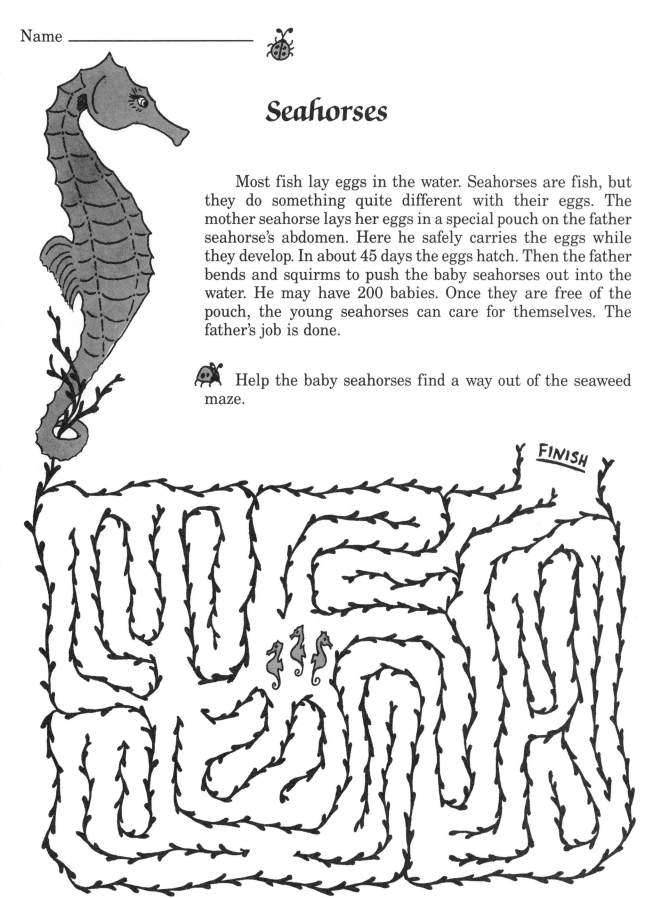

FINISH

Name _____

What Is a Fish?

There are more than 30,000 kinds of fish. They are found in lakes, rivers, streams, and deep, dark oceans. There are even fish living in caves thousands of feet underground. Fish are cold-blooded. This means that their bodies are the same temperature as the water around them.

Fish have 3 main body parts. They are the head, the body, and the tail. Most fish have scales except on their heads and fins. On large fish, the scales may be as big as your hand. On small fish, you may need a microscope to see their scales. The scales of a fish show rings of growth much like a tree stump. By counting the rings you can tell the fish's age.

The skull of a fish is protected by several bony plates. Some fish have teeth. Others have no teeth. A fish uses its tongue to touch things, but not to taste them. Fish have taste buds in their mouths and also on their skin!

Fish have two pairs of nostrils for smelling, but they are not used for breathing. A fish breathes through gills on both sides of its head. Oxygen from the water enters the fish's blood in its gills.

A fish has ears, but not like yours. A fish's ears have no outside openings. The fish's ears are for balance and for hearing vibrations in the water. Fish can move their eyes, but they have no eyelids to blink. Scientists believe that fish are nearsighted. The dark center or pupil of the eye is large to let in the light. The deeper under the water you go, the darker it gets. Fish probably can't see much anyway.

Most fish reproduce by spawning and laying eggs. A few, like some sharks, bear live young. Fish swim by moving their tails from side to side. The fins on their sides, backs, and bellies help them to steer and stay upright. Many fish have "swim bladders." A swim bladder is like a balloon in the center of the fish's body. By decreasing or increasing the amount of air in this bladder, the fish can rise or sink in the water.

Write "Yes" if the statement is true. If it is not true, write "No."

_____ 1. Fish are cold-blooded and breathe through gills.

_____ 2. A fish's ears have no outside openings.

_____ 3. Most kinds of fish have scales on their bodies.

_____ 4. The fins of a fish are like balloons.

_____ 5. Adult fish reproduce by spawning and laying eggs.

_____ 6. Fish use their nostrils for breathing and smelling.

Name

A Fish's Body

 On the drawing here, label the head, body, tail, eye, fins, gills, scales, and swim bladder.

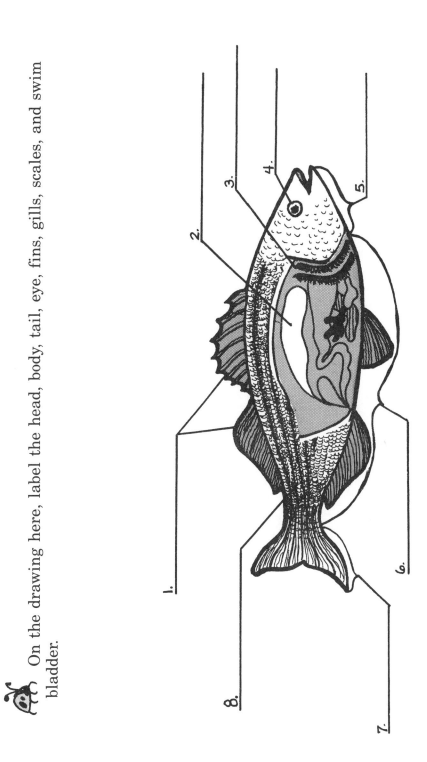

Name _____

All About Salmon

 Ready:

spawn
mysterious
journey
rapids
currents
bruised
redd
fertilizes
alevins
cycle

1. Something that happens, but we don't know why is _____.

2. A homonym for "red" is _____.

3. A place on your skin that turns black and blue is _____.

4. When fish lay eggs to produce offspring, we say that they

_____.

5. When salmon eggs hatch, the new little salmons are called

_____.

6. _____ are rocky areas in rough, fast-moving rivers.

 Set:

The salmon is one of the most common and interesting fish. Salmon spend most of their life in the sea. They remain in the salt water until they are ready to spawn. To spawn means to return to the fresh water where they were born and reproduce. Scientists do not know why or how the salmon knows when to make this mysterious trip. They call it the salmon's "homing instinct."

The salmon's journey home is long, difficult and dangerous. They struggle against strong river currents. They must fight their way over rapids and jump waterfalls. In some places people have built fish ladders around dams to help the salmon return home. Some salmon travel 2,000 miles. By the time they reach the spawning grounds they are bruised, starved, and close to dying.

Name _____

The female digs a nest by turning on her side and pushing away the gravel with her tail. She lays her eggs in the shallow nest called a redd. Salmon will lay up to 10,000 tiny pink eggs. After the male fertilizes the eggs, the female covers them with mud and plants.

Several months later the salmon eggs hatch. The newly-hatched salmon are called "alevins." After several more months they begin to look more like fish and are called "fry." When the fry are about 5 inches long, they begin the long trip to the sea. For protection, they swim at night and hide during the day. When these fry are adult salmon they will get the "homing instinct." They will make the difficult journey back to the spawning grounds and begin the cycle again.

 Go:

Salmon is one of the world's most important "food fish."

1. Salmon return to fresh water to spawn. (Yes, No)

2. When salmon first hatch they are called 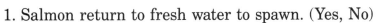.

3. Scientists know why and how salmon know when to make their long journey.

(Yes, No)

4. People have built _____ _____ around dams to help the salmon return to

the spawning grounds.

5. The (male/female) salmon digs the nest or redd.

The Derby

The fish at the bottom of the page were caught in the "Kids' Fishing Derby." The tag on each fish tells how much the fish weighs and who caught it. Use the tags to help answer the questions.

1. Who caught the largest fish? _____

2. How much did the smallest fish weigh? ____ pounds

   ____ ounces

3. Who caught a fish weighing 5 pounds 2 ounces? _____

4. How much did Andy's fish weigh? ____ pounds

   ____ ounces

5. Whose fish weighs 3 pounds 15 ounces? _____

Bonus

Number the prize ribbons to show which of the fish won 1st, 2nd, 3rd, 4th, and 5th places.

Name _____

How's the Weather?

As you read this story, circle the correct word in each numbered box at the bottom of this sheet.

Some people believe that the woodchuck or groundhog can predict the weather. The story goes that if the groundhog 1. _____ its shadow on February 2nd there will be 6 more weeks of winter weather. No one 2. _____ how this story started. Actually woodchucks 3. _____ or sleep all winter. They rarely leave their dens until early March.

The grizzly brown woodchuck is a 4. _____ of the rodent family. Like all rodents, groundhogs have special 5. _____ for gnawing. Their front incisor teeth keep growing all 6. _____ their lives. The woodchuck's gnawing keeps them worn down and chisel sharp.

An 7. _____ woodchuck is about the same size as a small dog. Groundhogs eat plants and live in 8. _____ they dig in the ground. Each groundhog 9. _____ has several entrances and may have 40 feet of underground tunnels.

You probably won't 10. _____ the groundhog's sharp whistle on February 2nd. Even so, many people still believe they are nature's weather forecasters.

1. sees hears eats	2. nos knows know	3. eat froze hibernate	4. adult primate member	5. ears teeth claws
6. in over of	7. adult baby little	8. burrows water trees	9. whistle den teeth	10. feel hear see

Name _____

"Classified" means "placed in a group."

Mammals

Mammals are warm-blooded and have backbones. They have fur or hair on their bodies. Most mammal babies are born alive. All animals whose young feed on milk from the mother are classified as mammals. Female mammals have special glands to produce milk to feed their babies. Mammals are the only animals that produce milk. This makes them easy to tell from all other animals.

There are more than 15,000 different kinds of mammals. Scientists believe that mammals have lived on the earth for more than 150,000,000 years. They live nearly everywhere in the world. You can find mammals in cold mountain areas and in the hottest deserts.

Scientists classify mammals into smaller groups. The members of each group have something about them that is alike. They all have certain body parts in common. Some have teeth alike. In one group all the mammals have pockets! Animals that seem very different may be grouped together. Grizzly bears and dogs are in the same group of meat-eaters.

Mammals are all shapes and sizes. The pigmy shrew weighs less than an ounce. A huge blue whale may weigh more than 100 tons. The tall giraffe, the whiskery walrus, and the flying bat are all mammals.

Write "Yes" by each true statement. If it is not true, put "No."

_____ 1. All mammals are large.

_____ 2. Mammals are warm-blooded and have backbones.

_____ 3. Most mammals hatch from eggs.

_____ 4. Only mammals produce milk to feed their young.

_____ 5. Most mammals have slick scales on their skin.

_____ 6. Mammals are classified by ways they are alike.

Name _____

Which Mammal Group?

Six common mammal groups are listed here. On the line below each animal's picture, write the name of its mammal group.

CAMEL   MONKEY   BEAR

1._____   2._____   3._____

Marsupials are mammals with pouches for carrying their young.
Rodents are gnawing mammals with sharp, chisel-shaped teeth.
Hoofed Animals are all mammals with hard hoof-like feet.
Carnivores are mammals that feed mostly on other animals' flesh.
Marine Mammals spend all or most of their lives in the sea.
Primates are the group of mammals most like man.

BEAVER   OPPOSUM   WHALE

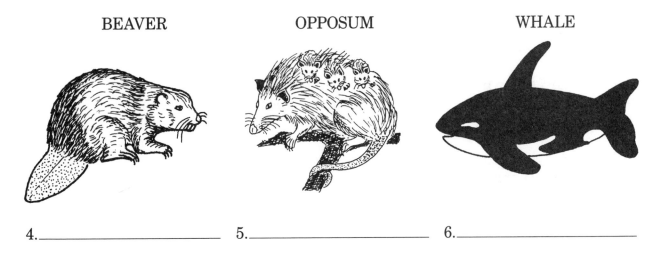

4._____   5._____   6._____

Name _____

All About the Platypus

 **Ready:**

similar
produce
leathery
sensitive
roots
burrow
winding
deposits
clutches
ooze

1. A word that rhymes with "boots" is _____.

2. A word that means the opposite of "different" is _____.

3. A hole dug in the ground by an animal is a _____.

4. Something that turns and twists is called _____.

5. _____ means "to seep or leak slowly."

Platypuses live in Australia and Tasmania.

 Set:

Most mammals are born alive. There are only two mammals that hatch from shells outside the mother's body. They are the anteater and the duckbilled platypus. Because they hatch from eggs, they are similar to reptiles. However, they are more like the mammals. They grow hair on their bodies and the females produce milk to feed their young.

The duckbilled platypus is a peculiar animal. It has a long flat tail like a beaver. Its webbed feet and bill are like a duck's, but a duck's bill is hard. The bill of a platypus is leathery and has sensitive nerves in it. The duckbilled platypus is an excellent swimmer and diver. It roots along river banks with its bill, digging up worms, crayfish, and grubs. When searching for food underwater, the platypus closes its eyes. It uses its senses of smell and touch to find its dinner.

Name _____

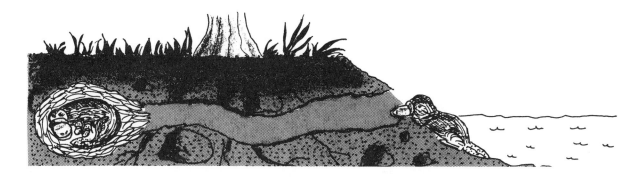

The female duckbilled platypus digs a winding tunnel into a riverbank. The nesting burrow can be 60 feet long. After she lines the nest with leaves, the mother platypus deposits two soft white eggs. Then she curls up and clutches her eggs to incubate them. Later, she cares for the young in the nest. Young platypuses feed by licking milk from the mother's fur. The milk oozes from pores on the mother's abdomen.

 Go:

1. A platypus is a (bird, reptile, mammal).

2. Where do platypuses live? _____ and _____

3. Platypuses are like reptiles because they _____ _____.

4. Most platypuses cannot see. (Yes, No)

5. How long can a nesting burrow be? _____ feet.

6. Platypuses have _____ and _____ like ducks.

Name _____

All About Chimpanzees

 Ready:

grasp
nimble
communicate
knuckle
upright
captivity
task
constantly
imitate

1. A job or work to be done is called a _____.

2. To grip or hold something in your hand is to _____it.

3. _____ is a compound word.

4. The word that begins with a silent letter is _____.

5. To talk with another person is a way to _____with him or her.

6. Another word that means almost the same as "copy" is

_____.

 Set:

Chimpanzees belong to the family of mammals called primates. Primates include the mammals that are most like man. In this group are apes, monkeys, gorillas, lemurs, and other animals. You are a primate.

Like all primates, chimpanzees have larger brains than the other mammals. Their bones are about the same in size and number as human bones. Their nimble hands look much like human hands. Like people, they have nails instead of claws on their fingers and toes. There is one big difference between the other primates and people. We use complicated language to think, plan, and communicate.

An adult chimpanzee is about 5 feet tall and weighs about 150 pounds. They have brown skin and straight black hair on most of their bodies. Their faces, ears, hands, and feet are pinkish in color. Usually chimpanzees walk on all fours by putting their weight on their knuckles, but they can also walk upright.

Name _____

Chimpanzees live in the rain forests. They spend their time searching the ground and trees for food. Young chimpanzees like to play just as much as human children do. About 20 chimpanzees usually live together in a "troop" or "band." We are constantly learning more about these animals. Scientists know chimpanzees can recognize shapes and basic colors. Some have even learned sign language. Because they love to imitate people, chimpanzees are often used as performers.

Chimpanzees are smart. They make and use simple tools to help with the task of finding food. A chimpanzee will make a branch into a "termite stick" and spend hours "fishing" for termites in the narrow holes of a termite nest.

A "primotologist" studies primates.

🐞 **Go:**

1. Primates are mammals most like _____.

2. A chimpanzee can walk upright. (Yes, No)

3. What tool can a chimpanzee make to help in gathering food? _____ _____

4. Chimpanzees can recognize shapes and basic _____.

5. Chimpanzees belong to the mammal group _____.

Name _____

Match the Critters!

Cut out the 12 triangles below. Match the animal halves. Paste the 6 animal pictures on another sheet of paper. Under each picture, write the name of the animal and its mammal group. Use the word box to help you.

pig	squirrel	primate
marine mammal		kangaroo
carnivore		hoofed animal
marsupial	fox	dolphin
	rodent	baboon

Name _____

A Killer Whale's dorsal fin can be as tall as a grown man!

Killer Whales

As you read this story, circle the correct word in each numbered box at the bottom of this sheet.

Many people believe the Orca or Killer Whale is a savage animal. Maybe this is because they don't know much 1. _____ Killer Whales.

A Killer Whale is 2. _____ to recognize by its black and white markings. The animal is mostly black with a 3. _____ belly and a white "saddle" patch on its back. The Killer Whale is the largest member of the dolphin family. An adult bull can be 4. _____ than 30 feet long and weigh 10 tons. Its tail fins or flukes may be 5. _____ across.

Killer Whales are excellent hunters. They can swim over 30 miles per hour. They use their sharp cone-shaped 6. _____ to catch fish, squid, and seals.

The Killer Whale lives and travels in family 7. _____ called pods. A pod may be 2 to 40 whales. Ten members is about average. The 8. _____ use clicks and high-pitched squeals to "talk" to one another. Killer Whales help each 9. _____ when in trouble. Pod members have been seen helping an injured whale stay afloat. They 10. _____ with the injured whale until it could swim alone. So you see, the Killer Whale may not always fit its name.

1. about as because	2. always easy hardly	3. green white purple	4. over into more	5. feet inches miles
6. claws eyes teeth	7. groups houses ways	8. fish people whales	9. other fish person	10. left stayed gone

Animal Families

Connect each animal to the names of its family members and then its group name. The first one is done for you.

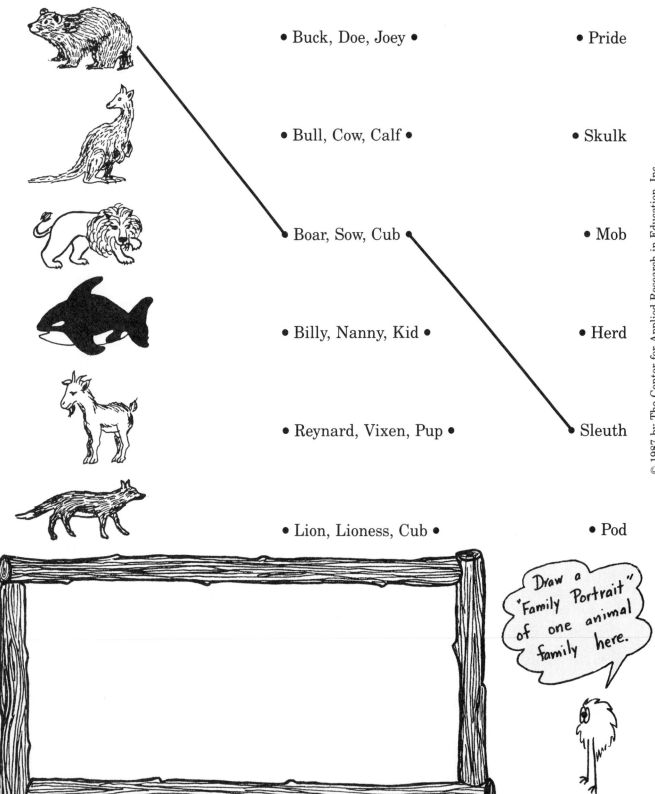

• Buck, Doe, Joey •   • Pride

• Bull, Cow, Calf •   • Skulk

• Boar, Sow, Cub •   • Mob

• Billy, Nanny, Kid •   • Herd

• Reynard, Vixen, Pup •   • Sleuth

• Lion, Lioness, Cub •   • Pod

Draw a "Family Portrait" of one animal family here.

The Great Race

Some of the animals decided to have a race to see who was fastest. Cat, Bat, and Ostrich were each sure that it could win. Snake and Fly each wanted to finish first, too. Although he had won a race with Hare once before, Tortoise knew all of the others could outrun him. Elephant and Whale thought they could win because they were biggest. Owl thought he could win because he was wisest. Duck just sat and quacked to himself, "I know I can't fly as fast as a golden eagle, but Eagle isn't here today."

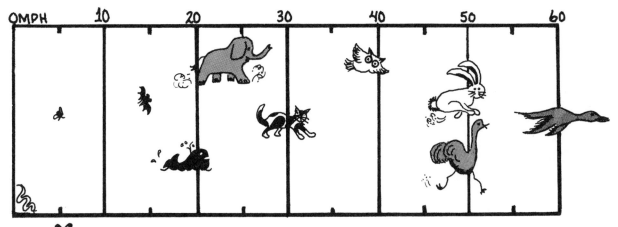

 Use the picture graph to help you answer these questions:

1. Which animals tied for 2nd place?_____ _____

2. How many miles per hour did the whale travel? _____mph

3. Was the elephant faster than the owl? _____

4. About how fast did the bat fly? _____mph

5. Which creature was slowest? _____

6. Look back in the story. The duck knew a bird who flew faster than he could fly. What kind of bird was that? _____

7. Who won the race? _____

A golden eagle can fly 120 mph!

Name _____

Animals Quick Check

Use the word box to help you complete the sentences.

milk	scales	feathers	air	gills
reptiles	hair	land	meat	snakes

1. Young mammals feed on _____ from their mothers.

2. Birds have _____ covering most of their bodies.

3. Crocodiles and alligators are _____.

4. Most mammals have _____ or fur covering their bodies.

5. Amphibians begin life in the water, but most adults live on the _____.

6. Reptiles have lungs, but fish have _____.

7. Mammals and birds breathe _____ just like reptiles.

Write "Yes" for true and write "No" for not true.

8. _____ Fish and reptiles have scales on their bodies.

9. _____ Animals in the mammal group are cold-blooded.

10. _____ All birds can fly.

11. _____ Insects have 3 body parts and 6 legs.

12. _____ Most marsupials lay eggs.

13. _____ A spider is not an insect.

14. _____ Most fish, birds, and reptiles lay eggs.

15. _____ A snake is an amphibian.

★Bonus: _____

What's your favorite animal?

Name —————————————

Bones and Muscles Word Search

Look for each of these words in the word search. The words can be found either across or down.

SKELETON

TENDONS

FEMUR

JOINTS

SKULL

RIBS

MUSCLES

BONES

AXIAL

VOLUNTARY

INVOLUNTARY

APPENDICULAR

```
                A F O
           H  N B K
      Q G P I C  J R
    Y B O D N F  T I
    Z V M L V E U S W
  N T U X B O N E S E G
  A B O S C S L R D I K H
  V C Y K P D U L E H G
  W B X A E Z Q N K M J F I
  J A V O L U N T A R Y L O
  W P A C E P X A Q M R N S
  B P U V T D T R E Y F Z G H
  I E S K O V M Y D O X A Q Z
  R U N J T N L W N E B P C Y
  G R D J T K U L V M W N X O
  Q H I S M U S C L E S Y P
  Z M B C N E O K G P I Q K
  L A R U D S F U T H U J
    V B X C L Y D G L F I K
      W A A X I A L Z E L H J
    L W X N A P B R C T D V
  B G J M Y O Z Q E S F U
  A L C O D N F F P S R I
  K T M U I J E E O G H Q
  W H K Y N T Z M C F E
  V J X I A T E B U G D
  L N R I B S N L R U C
  O M P G H D T A B
  D E F R Z O M Y
  Q I Y S N W
  X J K S
```

Name _____

Your Body's Framework

As you read this story, circle the correct word in each numbered box at the bottom of this sheet.

Your bones are your body's framework. Some 1. _____ support and shape your body. Other bones, like your skull 2. _____ ribs, help to protect soft organs including your brain, 3. _____, and lungs.

Your skeleton has two main parts. The bones of your head, 4. _____, and body are your axial skeleton. They 5. _____ the center of your body. The bones of your arms and legs attach 6. _____ your axial skeletons. Arm and leg bones 7. _____ up your appendicular skeleton.

Bones are different sizes and shapes. The tiniest bones are 8. _____ your ear. Your largest and strongest 9. _____ is your thigh bone or femur.

The human skeleton has more than 200 bones. We often 10. _____ of this framework as being very heavy. Actually the skeleton of a 150-pound person weighs only about 23 pounds!

About ½ of all your bones are in your hands and feet.

1. blood skin bones	2. not and under	3. toe heart hair	4. neck ear skin	5. is are was
6. to from away	7. make makes mark	8. inside to not	9. skin bone blood	10. think thank seem

Name _____

Mr. Bones

Glue this sheet to heavy paper and let it dry. Carefully cut out all pieces. Lay out your skeleton by matching the letters at each joint. The letters in gray circles go underneath. Fasten joints with small paper fasteners.

Name _____

You use 20 face muscles to smile.

Muscles and Tendons

You use 40 muscles to frown!

Muscles and tendons make your body work for you. They work together so that your body can move. You have more than 650 different muscles working for you.

There are 3 different types of muscles. They are skeletal muscle, smooth muscle, and heart muscle. Skeletal muscle covers the framework or skeleton of your body. Smooth muscle makes up the organs of your body such as your kidneys and stomach. Heart muscle controls the beating of your heart.

All types of muscles are divided into 2 groups. Voluntary muscles are muscles you can control. Skeletal muscles, like the ones in your arms and legs, are voluntary muscles. Involuntary muscles are muscles you cannot control. The heart muscles and smooth muscles are involuntary.

Skeletal muscles are attached to your bones by strong tendons. Tendons are tougher than muscle. Your strongest and thickest tendon is behind your ankle. You can feel this Achilles tendon, which attaches your lower leg muscle to your heel bone.

A person who weighs 150 pounds has about 60 pounds of muscle and 23 pounds of bones. More than half your weight is bones and muscles!

_____

Below are pictures of body parts. Under each part write "skeletal," "smooth," or "heart" to show its muscle type.

1.
—stomach

2.

3.

_____   _____   _____

Listed below are some body parts and some actions. Mark "V" on the line if the part or action uses voluntary muscles, and mark "I" for involuntary.

4. ____ stomach   8. ____ eyes
5. ____ waving   9. ____ running
6. ____ heart   10. ____ frown
7. ____ kidney   11. ____ tongue

Name _____

Label the Bones, Tendons, and Muscles

 On the drawing below, label the bones, tendons, and muscles.

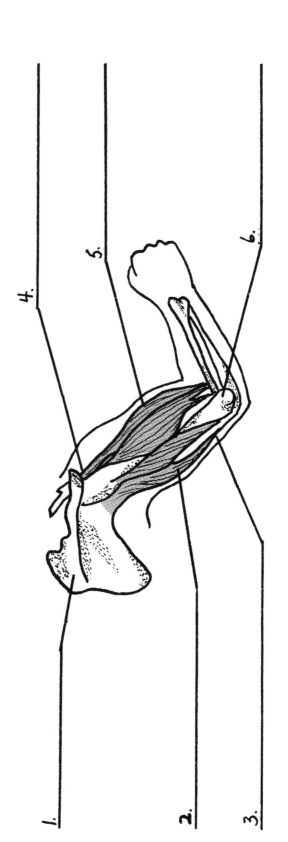

1.

2.

3.

4.

5.

6.

Name ______________________

Handwriting—Circulation

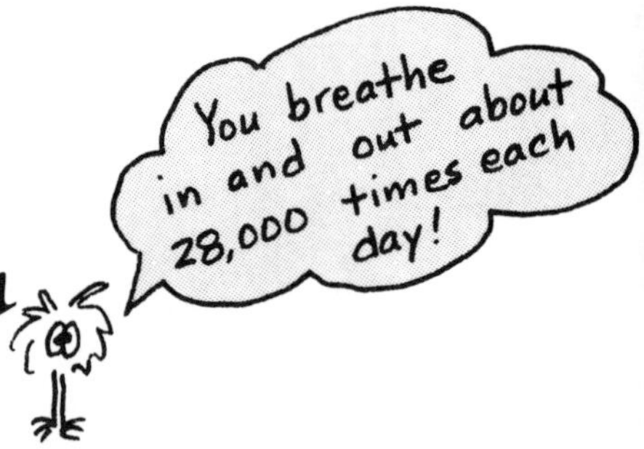
You breathe in and out about 28,000 times each day!

heart ______________________

____

lungs ______________________

____

blood ______________________

____

veins ______________________

____

arteries ______________________

____

capillaries ______________________

____

ventricle ______________________

____

atrium ______________________

____

oxygen ______________________

____

carbon dioxide ______________________

____

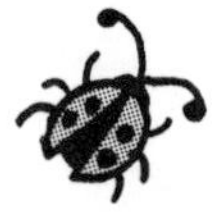

Name _____

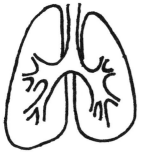

The Bellows

As you read this story, circle the correct word in each numbered box at the bottom of this sheet.

Night and day, asleep or awake, your bellows are working.

Your 1. _____ is constantly taking in oxygen and giving off carbon dioxide through 2. _____ lungs.

Air comes into your body through your 3. _____. Hairs and mucus help clean, warm, 4. _____ moisten the air. The wind pipe 5. _____ trachea passes air down into two bronchial tubes. One 6. _____ goes to your right lung and the other to your left lung.

Your bronchial tubes branch off into millions of tiny air sacs. These 7. _____ sacs are covered with very small blood vessels 8. _____ capillaries. Oxygen and carbon dioxide 9. _____ exchanged through the capillary walls.

When you inhale, your rib muscles and your diaphram contract. You can feel your 10. _____ move up and out. To exhale, the muscles relax. You feel your ribs move downward.

1. ears body legs	2. your my his	3. eyes nose ears	4. but and or	5. and or but
6. air lungs tube	7. air branch left	8. called not huge	9. are is was	10. nose ribs vessels

Name _____

Your Heart, Your Pump

The heart pumps blood to all parts of the body. The heart is a large hollow muscle about the size of your fist. It weighs less than one pound. Your heart is in the middle of your chest slightly toward your left side.

Your heart is made of strong muscle. When this muscle tightens and relaxes, blood is pumped through the body. You can hear or feel the pumping as your heartbeat. Your heart beats about 100,000 times every day!

Your heart has four sections called chambers. The two upper chambers are called atria. The two lower chambers are ventricles.

Oxygen-poor blood flows into the right atrium. It then moves to the right ventricle and is pumped to the lungs. Here the blood picks up oxygen. The oxygen-rich blood returns to the heart and enters the left atrium. From the left atrium the blood flows to the left ventricle and is pumped to the body. One complete round trip takes less than one minute. Your blood completes this trip more than 1,000 times each day!

 Look at the picture of the inside of a heart. Follow the directions below to trace the blood flow. You will need red and blue pencils or crayons.

1. Place your blue crayon on the place marked START.
2. Follow the arrows. Color in the blood flowing into the right atrium.
3. Continue down into the right ventricle and back up to the valve. (The valve keeps blood from flowing back.)
4. Continue with blue. Follow the arrows to the lungs.
5. Blood picks up oxygen in the lungs. Change to the red crayon to show oxygenated blood.
6. Color in along the arrows to show the blood return from the lungs. Continue into the left atrium.
7. Trace the path of blood into the left ventricle.
8. From the left ventricle, blood flows into the rest of your body.

Name _____

Picture of the Heart for "Your Heart, Your Pump"

★START★
FROM BODY

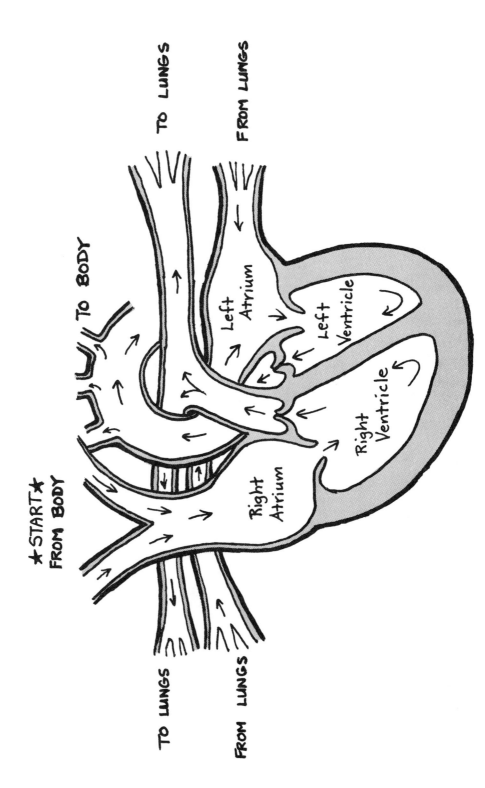

TO LUNGS

FROM LUNGS

TO BODY

Left Atrium

Left Ventricle

Right Ventricle

Right Atrium

TO LUNGS

FROM LUNGS

Name _____

Just Your Type

 **Ready:**

liquid supplies nourishment waste plasma platelets quart transfusion donor recipient	1. Two pints of liquid equals one _____. 2. Useless, unwanted material is called _____. 3. A _____ is someone who gives or donates. 4. Milk, water, and juice are _____ or fluid. 5. A _____ is someone who receives.

 Set:

Blood is the most important liquid in your body. The blood supplies oxygen and nourishment, removes waste, and helps your body repair itself and fight disease.

Blood is made up of a liquid called plasma. Plasma contains red cells that carry oxygen and give the blood its color. The white cells in blood kill germs and fight disease. Platelets cause blood to thicken and clot to stop bleeding from a wound. An adult has between 5 and 6 quarts of blood. If you weigh 50 pounds, you have about 1½ quarts of blood.

All races of people have one of four main blood types. Blood typing was discovered by Dr. Karl Landsteiner in the 1920s. He named the four types of blood A, B, AB, and O. For his discovery, he won a Nobel Prize in 1930.

Name _____

      If a person is very sick or badly injured, he or she may need a transfusion. This is when blood from one person is given to another. The person who gives the blood is a donor. The person who receives the blood is a recipient. Before a transfusion, doctors must match the donor's and recipient's blood. Blood cells that don't match will die.

      This chart shows the four blood types. Smiles mean the types match. Frowns mean they do not match. Use this chart to help you with some of the questions.

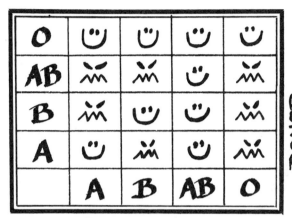

 Go:

1. The liquid part of blood is _____.

2. The first blood typing was done in the 1920s by _____.

3. _____, _____, _____, _____ are the 4 blood types.

4. A person of type B can receive blood from a type O donor. (Yes, No)

5. A person with type (A, B, O) can donate blood to all other types.

6. _____ are the cells that thicken the blood and clots to stop bleeding.

Name _____

Your brain weighs about 3 pounds

Your Brain

Your brain is your most important organ. It is a collector of information from every part of your body. Your brain controls your body functions, your memory, and even your emotions.

The three main parts of your brain are the cerebrum, the brain stem, and the cerebellum. The *cerebrum,* also called the forebrain, is wrinkled and dome-shaped. It lies toward the top and front of the skull. The cerebrum is divided into two hemispheres called cerebral hemispheres. The cerebrum contains nerve cells that have to do with intelligence, memory, and your ability to think and reason.

The *brain stem,* also called the midbrain, is between the cerebrum and the cerebellum. It contains the speech and hearing centers. Part of the brain stem, called the pons, controls messages to and from your body. The brain stem also works with vital organs such as your heart.

The *cerebellum* or hindbrain is toward the back and base of your skull. The cerebellum controls your balance and posture by receiving messages from your muscles, joints, and skin. The cerebellum also collects information from your eyes and ears and causes your body to respond automatically to new information.

On the line after each of the brain parts below write its other name. Below each part tell at least two of its special jobs.

1. Cerebrum: _____

_____

_____

_____

2. Brain Stem: _____

_____

_____

_____

3. Cerebellum: _____

_____

_____

_____

Name _____

Parts of the Brain

Here is a drawing of the side view of the brain. Label the cerebrum, brain stem, and cerebellum.

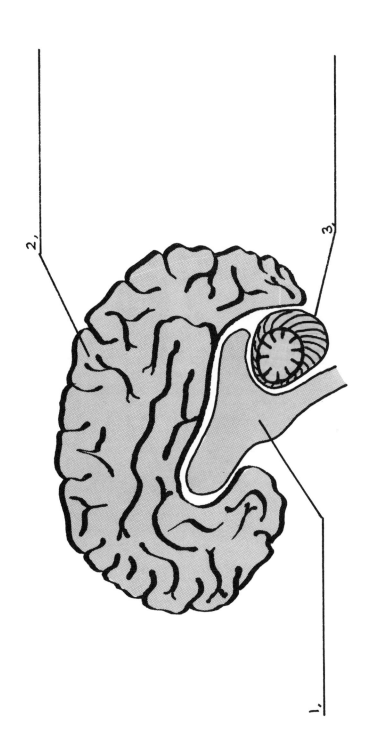

Name _____

What does an eye doctor do in the classroom?

Eyes

There are two basic parts to your eyes. The outer part holds the eye and protects it from injury. This outer part includes the boney socket, *eyebrow, eyelid, eye lashes,* and *tear ducts.* The other basic part of your eye is the "eyeball." It is shaped like a sphere and measures about one inch across. The eyeball is held in the socket by six muscles that allow the eye to move.

With a mirror, you can see some of the parts of your own eye. The tough, white outer covering is called the *sclera.* It covers the whole eye, but is transparent in the center. This center of the eye is the *cornea.* Just behind the cornea is the round, black opening called the *pupil.* The pupil lets light enter the inner eye. The colored area around the pupil is the *iris.*

Light rays enter the eye through the cornea and pupil. These rays are focused on the retina at the back of the eye. When light images strike the retina, they are upside down. This upside down image travels the optic nerve to the brain. Your brain then turns everything rightside up!

Examine the pupils!

Write "Yes" for each statement that is true. Write "No" for statements that are not true.

1. _____ Your eyeball is about one inch across.

2. _____ The outer part of your eye includes the retina.

3. _____ The iris is the colored part of your eye.

4. _____ The sclera is tough and white.

5. _____ Light rays enter the inner eye through the iris.

6. _____ The retina turns upside down light images rightside up.

7. _____ Six muscles hold your eye in the boney socket.

8. _____ Your eyeball is shaped like a sphere.

Name _____

Parts of the Eye

 Label the eyebrow, eyelid, eye lashes, tear ducts, sclera, cornea, pupil, and iris in the following drawing of the eye.

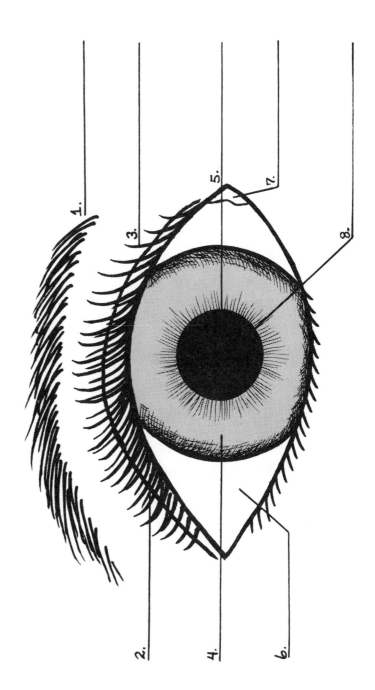

Name _____

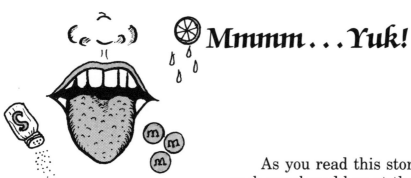

Mmmm...Yuk!

As you read this story, circle the correct word in each numbered box at the bottom of this sheet.

Your sense of taste comes from nerve cells just below the surface of your tongue. These 1. _____ cells called taste buds, send 2. _____ messages to your brain.

Four types of nerve 3. _____ are spread out over your tongue, but 4. _____ are not evenly spaced. Different parts of your 5. _____ are sensitive to different tastes. Some parts sense a salty taste, some sour, some sweet, and other parts 6. _____ bitterness.

Sometimes your tongue can't taste anything 7. _____ all. In order to taste something there must be moisture. The saliva in your 8. _____ allows your taste buds to work.

Your taste buds are a little different 9. _____ everyone else's. What is salty to you may seem bitter to someone 10. _____. This helps explain why people like different foods. It's all in your taste buds!

© 1987 by The Center for Applied Research in Education, Inc.

1. surface brain nerve	2. smell sound taste	3. tongue cells bud	4. it they this	5. brain tongue type
6. sense spread nerve	7. in at or	8. mouth brain tastes	9. this then than	10. other each else

Name _____

The Five Senses

 Next to each picture, list as many things as you can that appeal to that sense.

 _____
_____
_____
_____
_____
_____
_____

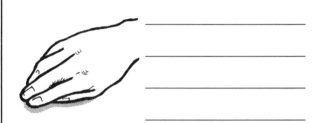(eye) _____
_____
_____
_____
_____
_____
_____

(nose) _____
_____
_____
_____
_____
_____

(hand) _____
_____
_____
_____
_____
_____

 _____
_____
_____
_____
_____
_____
_____

★ Describe one of your
favorite things. Use words
that appeal to your five
senses. _____
_____
_____
_____
_____

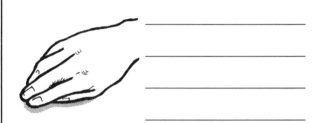

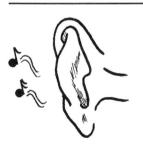

Name _____

More Than Just Sound

As you read this story, circle the correct word in each numbered box at the bottom of this sheet.

Ears are organs of hearing, but they do more than just hear. They 1. _____ help control your balance. Balance 2. _____ often called equilibrium.

There are three main 3. _____ to the ear. They are the ear drum, the small bones of the middle ear, 4. _____ the snail-shaped tube inside the ear. This tube, called the cochlea, has several thousand nerve cells and is 5. _____ with liquid. The nerves send sound messages to your 6. _____.

The cochlea also sends 7. _____ to the brain about equilibrium. Tip your head and the liquid in the cochlea presses harder on the 8. _____ on one side. Those nerves tell the brain that your 9. _____ is tipped. Spin around and the liquid 10. _____, too. When you stop, the liquid takes longer to stop. That's why you feel dizzy!

1. also and don't	2. is were are	3. parts ears drums	4. but nor and	5. empty under filled
6. ears brain feet	7. brains ears messages	8. nerves liquid drums	9. hand leg head	10. stops feels spins

Name _____

Fingerprints

Fingerprints are unique. No one has fingerprints exactly like yours. Even identical twins have different prints.

There are three basic patterns of fingerprints. An arch begins on one side and arches to the other side of your finger. A loop begins on one side, loops around the center and returns to the same side. A whorl forms a circular pattern in the middle of your finger.

Once you know these basic patterns you can examine your own fingerprints.

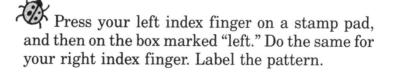 Press your left index finger on a stamp pad, and then on the box marked "left." Do the same for your right index finger. Label the pattern.

On the back of this page collect fingerprints from 5 of your friends. Label each fingerprint with the name of the person and the pattern of the print.

Name _____

All About Your Body's Outer Coat

 **Ready:**

| flexible |
| protective |
| epidermis |
| vessel |
| palm |
| sole |
| dermis |
| follicles |
| moist |
| sweat |

1. The bottom of your foot is called the _____.

2. _____ rhymes with "wet."

3. The outer layer of skin is the _____.

4. A word that means the opposite of "dry" is _____.

5. The roots from which hair grows are _____.

6. Your _____ is the inside surface of your hand.

 Set:

Your skin is a flexible, protective organ that covers your body. An adult's skin is about 16 square feet and weighs about 6 pounds!

Your skin has 2 layers. The epidermis is the outer layer. It is about as thick as 7 sheets of paper. The epidermis has some nerve cells but no blood vessels. This outer skin layer produces fingernails, toenails, and hair. The epidermis is thickest on your palms and the soles of your feet. Your eyelids have the thinnest skin layers of all.

Name _____

Below the epidermis is the layer called the dermis. In the dermis layer are nerves, glands, hair follicles, and blood vessels. When you scrape your elbow or knee, the epidermis layer is rubbed off and the dermis is exposed. This is why the scrape bleeds and hurts.

You have two kinds of glands in your skin. They are sweat glands and oil glands. Sweat glands help to regulate your body temperature. There are more than 2 million sweat glands in your skin.

The oil glands produce body oil that makes your hair shiny and keeps your skin moist. Oil glands are found near hair follicles. Along the hair follicles are muscles. These muscles make your hair stand up...like when you get "goose bumps."

 Go:

1. How many layers of skin do you have? _____

2. The outer layer of your skin is the _____ and the lower layer is the

_____.

3. Your skin is thickest on your eyelids and the soles of your feet. (Yes, No)

4. You have (2, 5, 7) million sweat glands in your skin.

5. When a scrape hurts and bleeds, the _____ is exposed.

6. _____ glands are found near the hair follicles.

Name _____

All About Germs

 **Ready:**

| germs |
| century |
| bacteria |
| organism |
| digest |
| disease |
| split |
| antibiotics |
| virus |
| multiply |

1. _____ is another word for "illness."

2. One hundred years make one _____.

3. Bacteria and viruses are both types of _____.

4. _____ are medicines that fight bacteria.

5. If you _____ something, you divide it in two.

 Set:

Do you wash your hands before you eat? Do you know why you should? You should wash because your hands are probably covered with germs!

Centuries ago, people believed that evil spirits caused disease. Today scientists know that many illnesses are caused by germs called bacteria and viruses.

Bacteria are tiny one-celled organisms that can only be seen through a microscope. Some bacteria are helpful, like the ones that help us digest food. Some bacteria are harmful. If you have ever had strep throat or pneumonia, you have had a disease caused by bacteria.

Name _____

Bacteria cells grow very rapidly by splitting. One cell splits into two. Those two cells split into four and so on. In just one day 16,000,000 cells may grow! Doctors use medicines called antibiotics to destroy bacteria infections.

Viruses are thousands of times smaller than bacteria. A virus can only be seen by using an electron microscope. Virus cells can't multiply by themselves the way bacteria do. Instead they take over other living cells and multiply rapidly. Colds, flu, mumps, measles, and chicken pox are all caused by viruses.

Now you know about germs. When lunch is ready—wash your hands!

Germs really bug me!

 Go:

1. Scientists know that many diseases are caused by _____ called bacteria and viruses.

2. Some bacteria are helpful. (Yes, No)

3. Pneumonia is caused by _____.

4. _____ cells grow rapidly by splitting.

5. Colds, flu, and chicken pox are all caused by _____.

6. Centuries ago people believed _____caused diseases.

7. Doctors use _____to destroy bacteria.

Name _____

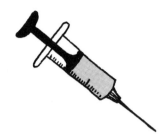

Why Get Shots?!

As you read this story, circle the correct word in each numbered box at the bottom of this sheet.

© 1987 by The Center for Applied Research in Education, Inc.

Nearly everyone has had a shot. Almost no one likes 1. _____. Then what is in them and why do we 2. _____ shots?

Immunization shots are special injections 3. _____ help to prevent diseases. You get a 4. _____ to keep you from getting a certain illness.

Immunization shots contain vaccines. A vaccine is made from a 5. _____ small amount of the germ that causes a disease. When a vaccine is 6. _____ into your body, disease-fighters called antibodies grow. These antibodies guard 7. _____ against the disease.

Most children get at least two 8. _____ of shots. One kind guards against measles, mumps, and rubella. The 9. _____ is for diptheria, pertussis, and tetanus.

When your parents were children, 10. _____ also got a vaccination against smallpox. This vaccine worked so well that no one has gotten the disease for many years. Children don't even need smallpox vaccinations any more!

1. what everyone shots	2. get got go	3. that who those	4. shot disease special	5. many very huge
6. lost dropped injected	7. me you them	8. disease different kinds	9. measles children other	10. he they she

Name _____

How Do You Measure Up?

Use a measuring tape to find the measurements. You may need a friend's help. Be sure to label in inches or centimeters.

1. I am _____ tall.

2. It is _____ around my head.

3. My thumb is _____ long.

4. My right foot is _____ long.

5. From my shoulder to the tip of my little finger is _____.

6. My left ankle is _____ around and my right ankle is _____ around.

7. It is _____ around my left knee.

8. My nose is _____ long.

9. My middle is _____ around.

10. It is _____ around my right elbow.

 If you and your friend lay down head-to-head, how far would his or her feet be from yours? (Hint: Use addition)

 _____

Name _____

Human Body Quick Check

 Use the word box to help you complete the sentences.

heart	brain	skin	blood	tendons
stomach	liver	muscles	skeleton	lungs

1. Your bones make up your _____.

2. Muscles and _____ work together to make your body move.

3. Smooth, skeletal, and heart are all different types of _____.

4. Your body takes in oxygen through your _____.

5. Your _____ pumps blood to all of your body.

6. The four main _____ types are A, B, AB, and O.

7. The _____ is a collector of information from every part of your body.

Write "Yes" for true and write "No" for not true.

8. _____ The cerebellum is part of your heart.

9. _____ Your eyeball is shaped like a sphere.

10. _____ Everyone's taste buds are exactly the same.

11. _____ Your nose controls your equilibrium.

12. _____ Fingerprints can have arches, loops, or whorls.

13. _____ The epidermis is a layer of your skin.

14. _____ Viruses and bacteria can cause disease.

15. _____ An immunization shot can guard against disease.

Section Three

EARTH SCIENCE
ACTIVITIES

Geology Word Search

Look for each of these words in the word search. The words can be found either across or down.

```
        O  X  E  A  L  I  V
        P  N  W  B  D  K  U  M
     T  C  R  U  S  T  B  H  C  Q
  J  S  O  K  J  A  C  H  L  F  B  P  A  O  E
  R  I  R  G  F  Z  C  G  I  D  L  M  K  A  J  I
  L  P  Q  E  M  B  Y  D  D  Q  E  I  O  P  N  E  O  G
  Q  H  R  J  A  C  H  E  F  U  E  Q  M  L  F  L  M  O
G  L  M  E  O  N  K  I  V  G  I  N  U  P  A  O  O  M  C  U
F  O  M  W  K  T  L  A  I  T  D  U  Q  F  N  S  E  A  L  K  O
A  N  F  G  E  O  L  O  G  Y  G  R  S  I  H  E  S  I  G  Q  I  N
B  E  X  S  F  A  E  G  W  O  M  A  G  N  E  T  I  S  M  Y  N  P
N  O  C  E  V  B  J  Y  U  X  I  H  J  Z  A  P  L  A  W  R  E  U
P  E  D  U  C  D  G  I  S  O  L  I  D  F  J  M  X        A  S  T
Y  R  Q  U  G  R  A  V  I  T  Y  L  G  K                    V
T  A  B  D  A  C  H  Z  Y  B  E  C
Z  R  E                    A  D
S
```

CRUST	ERA	LIQUID	MAGNETISM
MANTLE	EON	SOLID	GEOLOGY
FOSSIL	CORE	PLANET	GRAVITY

Name _____

How Big Is Small?

The earth weighs 6,600,000,000,000,000,000,000 tons!

As you read this story, circle the correct word in each numbered box at the bottom of this sheet.

You live on the planet Earth. Our earth is made of 1. _____, land, and air. About 3/4 of the earth's surface is covered by water and ice. This is the hydrosphere. The land, called the biosphere, covers about 1/4 of the 2. _____. The air surrounding the earth is the atmosphere.

Most 3. _____ think the earth is a round ball. This is almost true. The earth is not really perfectly round. 4. _____ is slightly flatter at the poles and fatter at 5._____ equator.

The earth is a small planet. Just how big is a small 6. _____? The earth is 7. _____ 25,000 miles around. If the equator were a freeway and you could circle the globe at 60 mph, it would take more than 2½ weeks to drive 8. _____ once. That's if you didn't stop to eat, sleep, or go to the bathroom!

To make a tunnel 9. _____ the earth's center to the other side, you would have to 10. _____ 8,000 miles. That is as far as from New York to California—4 times!

1. water dirt sky	2. moon earth sun	3. planets people animals	4. It They She	5. these those the
6. planet moons sun	7. many about some	8. through around under	9. out through back	10. fly climb dig

Crust, Mantle, Core

...and atmosphere, too!

Geologists believe that the earth is made up of layers. The earth has four layers: the core, the mantle, the crust, and the atmosphere.

The layers of the earth are something like the layers of a peach. The fuzz surrounding the peach is like the earth's *atmosphere*. The part of the earth we live on is the crust. The *crust* covers the earth much like skin covers the peach. The skin on the peach is very thin, but the earth's crust is between 5 and 30 miles thick. Around us, we see soil, rocks, mountains, deserts, and oceans. All of these are part of the earth's crust.

Under its skin, a peach has soft flesh. Under the earth's crust is the *mantle*. The mantle is about 1,800 miles thick. It is made of rock, but it is not hard. The mantle is soft and thick like taffy. The mantle moves very slowly. It moves because some parts of the mantle are hot while other parts are cooler. Movement causes changes in the earth. Sometimes we feel these changes as earthquakes or volcanic eruptions.

Deep inside the earth, like the pit in the peach, is the earth's core. Scientists believe the *core* has two parts. The outer core is very hot molten metal. In the center of the core, about 4,000 miles below us, is a solid ball of metal.

 Write "Yes" if the statement is true. Write "No" if the statement is not true.

1. _____ The crust of the earth is about 50 miles thick.

2. _____ The earth has four layers.

3. _____ The earth's outside layer is the mantle.

4. _____ The outside of the core is hot liquid metal.

5. _____ The mantle of the earth is soft and thick like taffy.

6. _____ Movement in the core of the earth causes earthquakes and volcanic eruptions.

7. _____ A solid ball of metal is inside the core.

8. _____ The mantle is made of rock.

9. _____ Rocks, mountains, and valleys are part of the earth's atmosphere.

10. _____ We live on the crust of the earth.

Name _____

Parts of the Earth

 Label the atmosphere, the crust, the mantle, and the core in this drawing of the earth.

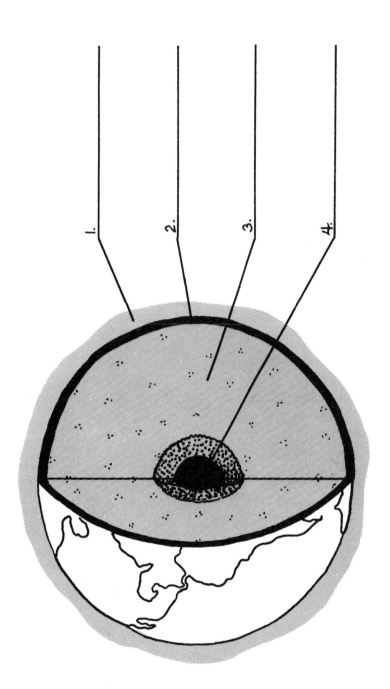

1.

2.

3.

4.

Name _____

All About Magnetism

 **Ready:**

| century |
| ancient |
| attracted |
| magical |
| compass |
| navigate |
| opposite |
| rotates |
| equator |
| constantly |

1. The imaginary mid-line of the earth is the _____.

2. The word that means "mysterious" or "supernatural" is

_____.

3. If two things are drawn together, they are _____.

4. A _____ is 100 years.

5. Antonyms are words that mean the _____ of each other.

6. If something _____, it spins around and around.

 Set:

The first magnets were discovered more than 2,000 years ago. Shepherds in an ancient country called Magnesia found that certain rocks stuck to the iron ends of their staffs. These hard, black lodestones had a pulling power that attracted metal. Many people thought lodestones were magical.

Centuries later people discovered another amazing thing about lodestones. A piece of lodestone hung on a string would turn so its ends pointed north and south. Later lodestone compasses were made to help sailors navigate.

Name _____

The magnets we use today are very much like lodestones. Our magnets have two opposite poles. The north pole and the south pole of a magnet are of equal strength. We know that two like magnetic poles repel or push against each other. We also know that opposite poles attract each other. The space around a magnet is called the magnetic field.

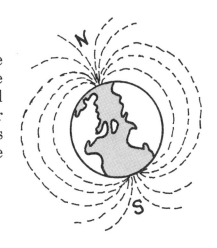

The largest magnet is the Earth. Our planet is like a giant magnet. It has a magnetic north pole and a magnetic south pole. The magnetic field around the earth is constantly changing as the earth rotates. Electrical energy moves from the core of the earth to the poles. The magnetism is strongest at the poles.

No one knows what exactly causes magnetism. The shepherds were amazed by lodestones. We are still amazed by the largest magnet—our Earth.

 Go:

1. Magnets were first discovered (200, 100, 2,000) years ago by shepherds in Magnesia.

2. The first magnetic rocks were called _____.

3. A _____ helps sailors to navigate their ships.

4. The space around a magnet is the _____.

5. The magnetic pull of the earth is strongest at the two _____.

6. Our largest magnet is the _____.

Name _____

Mysterious Gravity

As you read this story, circle the correct word in each numbered box at the bottom of this sheet.

Gravity pulls everything toward the center of the earth. When you jump, gravity 1. _____ you back down. Gravity is what "holds" things on the Earth. Gravity is everywhere on the 2. _____, but we can't see it. We can only 3. _____ what it does.

We can measure 4. _____ with a scale. The more something weighs, the more gravity is pulling on it. Do you know how much gravity 5. _____ on you? If you weigh 75 6. _____, that is how much gravity is pulling on you.

The farther you 7. _____ from the Earth's center, the less gravity pulls on you. Astronauts can become "weightless" in space because they are 8. _____ from the earth's gravitational pull.

Other planets 9. _____ gravity, too. Some have more and some have less gravity than the Earth. If you 10. _____ 75 pounds here, you would weigh about 12 pounds on the moon. On Jupiter you would weigh nearly 200 pounds!

1. lifts makes pulls	2. air Earth oceans	3. have see makes	4. gravity push lift	5. pushes lifts pulls
6. ounces tons pounds	7. see are fall	8. near far over	9. has have were	10. drops picked weigh

Name _____

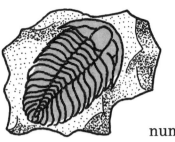

Ancient Prints

As you read this story, circle the correct word in each numbered box at the bottom of this sheet.

Have you ever looked for fossils? Fossils are the 1. _____ remains or prints of plants and animals preserved in rock. Fossils 2. _____ found in sedimentary rock such as shale or limestone. You can probably 3. _____ fossils in an area near where you live.

Millions of 4. _____ ago, plants and animals were buried in the sediment of swamps, 5. _____, and oceans. The soft parts of these animals and plants decayed. 6. _____ or silt filled in the empty spaces of the skeletons that remained. More 7. _____ of sediment built up. The layers were squeezed together by the weight of the water on top. This pressure turned the layers to solid 8. _____.

As millions of years passed, the Earth changed. Pressures 9. _____ in the Earth slowly pushed the rock up and out of the water. Fossils once formed beneath the ocean are now on 10. _____ land. The fossils of ancient sea animals can even be found on high mountainsides.

1. new ancient wet	2. are is am	3. lose hear find	4. years days months	5. mountains air lakes
6. Water Mud Plants	7. layers swamps water	8. water dirt rock	9. over side deep	10. an the these

Name _____

The Earth's Story

The earth's story began billions of years ago. No one knows the exact age of the earth. Geologists learn about the early history of the earth from rock formations. Fossils are some of the oldest records of the earth's history.

A billion is one thousand millions! WOW!

Geologists use a geologic time scale to talk about the history of the earth. A geologic time scale is like a timeline. You could make a timeline of your life showing important events and dates. Your timeline would be short, because you are young. The earth's timeline is billions of years long.

Scientists divide the earth's history into two eons. The first eon lasted about 4 billion years. We know little about this first eon. No traces of living things are left for scientists to explore.

We know more about the second eon, which scientists divide into three eras. An era is a length of time like an eon, but much shorter. The first era, called the Paleozoic Era, began about 520 million years ago. During this time, small marine animals like worms, jellyfish, and fish with backbones lived in the oceans and seas.

The second era, the Mesozoic Era, began about 185 million years ago. This was the time of the great reptiles. Dinosaurs ruled the land. Many fossils remain today to tell the story of the Mesozoic Era.

Sixty million years ago, the Cenozoic Era began. We are now living in this era. Mammals have come to rule in this era. You are a creature of the Cenozoic Era!

Below write the names of three animals that scientists believe lived in each era.

Paleozoic Era	Mesozoic Era	Cenozoic Era
1. _____	4. _____	7. _____
2. _____	5. _____	8. _____
3. _____	6. _____	9. _____

© 1987 by The Center for Applied Research in Education, Inc.

Name _____

The Phanerozoic Eon

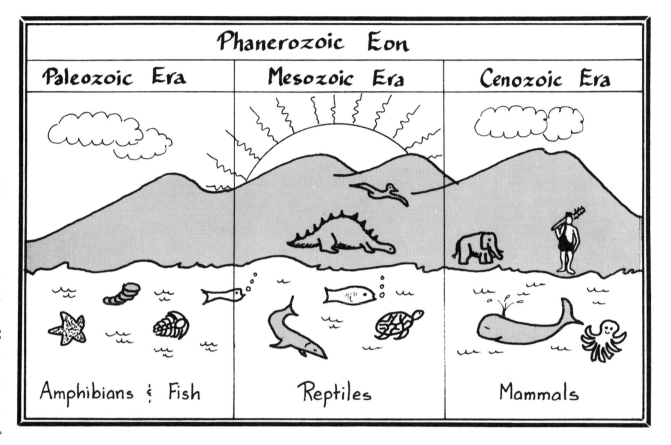

On each line write "Yes" if the statement is true. If the statement is false write "No."

1. _____ Geologists learn about the earth from rocks.

2. _____ Man is part of the earth's Cenozoic Era.

3. _____ Dinosaurs were the first creatures on the earth.

4. _____ A geologic time scale is very short.

5. _____ Eons and eras are long periods of time.

Name _____

All About Radiocarbons

 **Ready:**

radioactive creatures absorb radiocarbons rays remaining archaeologist decays carbon prehistoric

1. Which two words rhyme with "days"? _____, _____.

2. A person who studies ancient things is an _____.

3. Something that happened before recorded history is

   _____.

4. If something gives off energy or rays, it is _____.

5. Another word for "animals" is _____.

6. _____ means "left."

 Set:

One of the ways scientists find out how old things are is radioactive carbon dating. Scientists use this dating test in their study of prehistoric creatures.

Radiocarbons are formed in the cosmic rays of our earth's atmosphere. These radiocarbons are absorbed by all living things. All plants and animals absorb radiocarbons. You do, too!

Radiocarbons give off rays called radioactivity. When something dies, it stops taking in radiocarbons. As the thing decays, it loses radiocarbons. Scientists can measure the rays and tell how old something is by how much radioactivity is left. Scientists know that something loses half of its radioactivity in about 5,600 years. Every 5,600 years, it loses half of its remaining radiocarbons.

Name _____

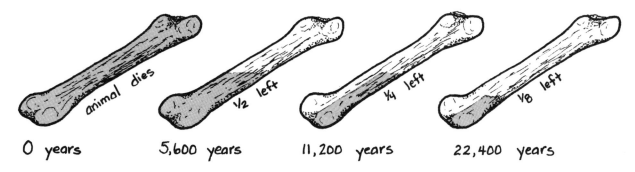

0 years   5,600 years   11,200 years   22,400 years

Let's try an example. An archaeologist digs up a bone. She thinks it may have come from a dinosaur. Radiocarbon dating can help her find out.

When the bone was part of a living animal, it absorbed radiocarbons. When the creature died, the bone began to decay. It has been losing radioactivity for thousands of years. Our archaeologist heats a small piece of the bone. The bone burns until nothing is left but pure carbon. By measuring the rays given off by the carbon, she can tell that the bone is old enough to have come from a prehistoric animal.

A "Geiger Counter" counts radioactive rays.

 Go:

1. Radiocarbons give off _____ called radioactivity.

2. All plants and animals _____ radiocarbons while they are alive.

3. When something dies it decays and gives off radioactivity. (Yes, No)

4. Something loses about _____ of its radioactivity in about 5,600 years.

5. Radiocarbon dating helps scientists to tell how (heavy, strong, old) something is.

Name ———————————————————

Name It!

Cut apart the squares on the dark lines. Unscramble them to make a picture of an animal from the Mesozoic Era. Glue the picture to another piece of paper and color it.

Use an encyclopedia or library book to help you complete these sentences. Write the finished paragraph on the other paper below your picture.

This is a picture of a 1. ——————. This "roof lizard" lived about 2. ——————

years ago during the Mesozoic Era. The 3. —————— was about 4. —————— long

and weighed about 5. ——————. This plated dinosaur looked fierce, but did not have

strong teeth and probably ate 6. ——————.

Name _____

How Much Do You Weigh?

Places	Pounds
Earth	50
Moon	8
Mars	19
Saturn	57
Neptune	71
Sun	13,950

All of the planets in our solar system have gravity. However, they do not have the same amount of gravity. Suppose you weigh 50 pounds on Earth. This chart tells what you would weigh in some other places.

Depends— on where you are !!!

 Use the chart to help you answer the questions.

1. How much would you weigh on Neptune?_____

2. How much would you weigh on the Moon?_____

3. On which place would you weigh most?_____

4. Where would you weigh the least?_____

5. On which place would you weigh nearest to what you weigh on Earth?_____

6. On how many planets would you weigh more than you weigh on Earth?_____

7. On how many places would you weigh less than you weigh on Earth?_____

Name _____

Handwriting—Geology

Geology is the study of the earth. When you study the earth you are a Geologist.

geologist _____

erosion _____

glacier _____

volcano _____

earthquake _____

mountain _____

igneous _____

sedimentary _____

metamorphic _____

geyser _____

Name _____

A Rock Story

As you read this story, circle the correct word in each numbered box at the bottom of this sheet.

There are large rocks and small rocks, bumpy rocks and smooth rocks. Some 1. _____ have beautiful colors and others are just plain ordinary. But when we talk about how they were made, there are 2. _____ three kinds of rocks.

Igneous rocks are the oldest 3. _____ of rocks. The word "igneous" 4. _____ "fiery." Igneous rocks are formed by the cooling 5. _____ hardening of very hot molten rock. Granite and pumice are igneous rocks.

Rocks formed by the settling of materials on land or in water 6. _____ sedimentary rocks. Over millions of 7. _____ sand, shells, and clay turn to solid rock. Sedimentary rocks often show layers. Fossils are sometimes 8. _____ in sedimentary rock.

Metamorphic rocks are the third type of 9. _____. Metamorphic means "to change form." These rocks were once igneous or sedimentary. They were 10. _____ by heat, pressure, or chemicals. Marble and agate are metamorphic rocks.

1. smooth rocks bumps	2. just many some	3. rock kind fire	4. means is does	5. but either and
6. is can are	7. days months years	8. found under show	9. clay rocks solids	10. settling changed either

Name _____

What Makes Mountains?

Geologists call any land area rising 2,000 feet above the land around it a mountain. Mountains are formed in four ways, but all are caused by movements in the earth's crust. *Folded mountains* are found along coastlines. Here forces push upward and sideways  to form folds in the earth's surface. The Appalachian Mountains in the eastern United States are folded mountains.

In some places the earth's crust has been broken, bent, and crumpled into huge blocks. Some blocks move down or up, or are tilted. These mountains are *fault or block mountains*. The Sierra Nevada Mountains are block mountains.

Dome mountains occur when molten rock cannot break through the earth's surface. Instead it spreads out in layers under the surface. This causes the surface to rise like a blister. South Dakota's Black Hills are dome mountains.

Volcanic mountains form along cracks in the earth's crust. Lava, rock, ash, and gases erupt through the crack in the earth. Many layers build up to form volcanic mountains. The Cascade Mountains of Washington and Oregon are volcanic mountains.

Mountains cover about ⅕ of all our land area. Some are big and some not so big. Are there mountains near where you live?_____

Name _____

More About Mountains

On the lines, tell how each range was formed.

1. Appalachian Mountains _____

_____

2. Sierra Nevada Mountains _____

_____

3. Black Hills _____

_____

4. Cascade Mountains _____

_____

5. Label the four mountain ranges on the map.
6. Draw a star on the map to show about where you live.
7. What type of mountains are nearest to where you live? _____

All About Mount St. Helens

 **Ready:**

erupted
tremors
spurts
bulge
pumice
pyroclastic
mudflow
destroyed
vanished
approximately
perish
midst

1. We don't know the exact number, so we say

_____ how many.

2. (Pumice, Pyroclastic, Mudflow) is glasslike ash.

3. The word with the same "or" sound as "doctor" is _____.

4. _____ is a compound word.

5. A word that rhymes with "hurts" is _____.

6. _____ means the opposite of "survive."

7. Another word for "a rounded bump" is _____.

 Set:

Scientists studied, measured, recorded, and photographed Mt. St. Helens for months. This beautiful mountain had been quiet for 123 years. Now there were earthquakes, minor eruptions, tremors, and spurts of steam. A large bulge was growing on the mountainside. A major eruption would soon occur.

On May 18, 1980, Mt. St. Helens, in the state of Washington, erupted. At 8:32 on Sunday morning, a huge blast was felt over 200 miles away. The mountaintop was gone. Steam, poisonous gases, and rocks as big as trucks spewed from the crater. Pumice, ice blocks, and pyroclastic glasslike ash were thrown 12 miles high.

Name _____

BULGE
8:27:00 a.m.

BLAST
8:32:41 a.m.

SURGE
8:32:51 a.m.

In 4 minutes, the ash cloud was 20 miles wide. The sky turned gray, then black as the cloud moved across the Northwest. Town after town was buried in ash and darkness. In some areas, 3 feet of snowlike ash fell in just 90 minutes.

The total eruption lasted 9 hours. Floods and mudflows destroyed the forests. Over 200 square miles of trees vanished. Approximately 60 people were killed. Two million birds and animals perished and 26 lakes were destroyed.

Scientists still watch as the mountain continues to rumble. It will take years for the land to recover, but there are signs of new life. In the midst of the destruction, plants are sprouting through the ash. Animals and birds are also beginning to return to Mt. St. Helens.

 Go:

1. Before 1980, how long had Mt. St. Helens been quiet? _____

2. The word _____in paragraph 4 means "disappeared."

3. In just 1½ hours, 3 feet of ash fell like snow in some places. (Yes, No)

4. Mt. St. Helens is in the state of _____.

5. Scientists study, measure, _____, and photograph Mt. St. Helens.

6. On May 18, 1980, the eruption lasted 9 hours. (Yes, No)

Name _____

Volcanoes

As you read this story, circle the correct word in each numbered box at the bottom of this sheet.

Every volcano begins with a crack or weak spot in the earth's crust. The crack reaches down 1. _____ the earth to a pocket of hot melted rock. This thick, doughy, melted 2. _____ is called magma. The magma is slowly pushed to the 3. _____ by pressure inside the earth.

When you open a soda can that 4. _____ been shaken you see the release of pressure. Foam and soda squirt 5. _____ the can. The earth's pressure is released in a volcanic 6. _____. Magma bulges out into a volcanic cone. The saucer shape at the top is 7. _____ the crater. Magma, now called lava, pours from the crater.

Scientists divide 8. _____ into three groups. The active volcanoes are erupting now or could 9. _____ soon. Dormant or sleeping volcanoes may have erupted recently, but show no activity now. Extinct volcanoes have not erupted for a 10. _____ long time and probably will not erupt again. There are several thousand extinct volcanoes, but only about 850 active ones.

© 1987 by The Center for Applied Research in Education, Inc.

1. outside inside over	2. ice rock crack	3. surface core earth	4. have won't has	5. from under over
6. crack bulge eruption	7. not seen called	8. bulges volcanoes cracks	9. push erupt divide	10. much very little

Name _____

Geysers

As you read this story, circle the correct word in each numbered box at the bottom of this sheet.

Geysers are very much like volcanoes. They are 1. _____ created by heat inside the earth. When a volcano erupts, hot melted rock 2. _____ into the air. Geysers shoot hot water and steam.

When water seeps into a deep narrow crack in the earth's 3. _____, it is heated by the hot rock below. When the water becomes hot enough to form steam, pressure builds up. The 4. _____ forces water and steam back up the crack. The geyser erupts, spouting high into the 5. _____.

"Old Faithful" is the most famous 6. _____ in the United States. It is one of over 200 geysers in Yellowstone National Park. The geyser earned the name "Old Faithful" 7. _____ it erupts regularly every 65 minutes. Few geysers are so regular in their eruptions. Just before each 8. _____ there is a rumbling sound in the earth. Then a hissing sound follows as the 9. _____ and steam rush to the surface. After spouting about 15,000 gallons of water over 120 feet into the air, the 10. _____ is quiet. "Old Faithful" is building up steam for another eruption.

1. both neither some	2. seeps falls shoots	3. core skin crust	4. dirt pressure crack	5. water air steam
6. volcano geyser crack	7. because but until	8. day eruption rumble	9. rock earth water	10. geyser volcano steam

Name _____

All About Rivers of Ice

 **Ready:**

| glacier |
| compact |
| erode |
| pressure |
| advance |
| flow |
| surface |
| scooping |
| sediment |
| ancient |

1. A word that rhymes with "go" is _____.

2. Something that is very, very old could be called _____.

3. The word with the same "oo" sound as "tool" is _____.

4. _____ means "to wear away something."

5. Something made smaller by pressure is _____.

6. A river of ice is a _____.

 Set:

The word "glacier" comes from the French word "glacé" which means "ice." A glacier forms where more snow falls than melts. Slowly the snow changes into rock-hard ice. When you squeeze a snowball, the heat from your hand softens the snow. As you squeeze air out, the snowball becomes hard and compact. In much the same way, changing temperatures and pressure from more snow form the glacial ice.

There are two kinds of glaciers. The largest glaciers are called ice sheets. Antarctica is covered by an ice sheet. In places the ice covering may be more than 2 miles thick!

The most common glaciers are valley glaciers. Like rivers of ice, valley glaciers move down mountainsides. Most glaciers move only 1 or 2 feet each day. A very "fast" glacier may move 10 feet in a day. Because they advance so slowly, action of glaciers on the Earth's surface may take thousands of years.

Like a river, a glacier flows over the land, scooping out boulders, rocks, gravel, and dirt. When the glacier melts, it deposits its load of sediment. These deposits change the land surface. In this way, glaciers wear down or erode some areas and later build up other areas. You can see the work of ancient glaciers today. Niagara Falls, Minnesota's "land of ten thousand lakes," and the Great Salt Lake were all formed by the action of glaciers.

An iceberg is a chunk of glacier that broke off into the sea.

 Go:

1. The most common kind of glacier is called _____ _____.

2. Glacier action builds up and wears away the Earth's surface. (Yes, No)

3. "Glacier" comes from a French word that means _____.

4. What continent is covered by an ice sheet? _____

5. Glaciers usually move 1 to 2 miles per day. (Yes, No)

6. Pressure and changing _____ change snow into glacial ice.

Name _____

80% of all earthquakes occur in the "Ring of Fire."

Earthquakes

As you read this story, circle the correct word in each numbered box at the bottom of this sheet.

An earthquake is caused when energy is released from inside the earth. Earthquakes can open cracks in the 1. _____ or loosen rocks and trees. They can even destroy buildings or cause tidal waves.

If you bend a stick, for a while 2. _____ will bend under the pressure. Suddenly the 3. _____ is too strong and the stick snaps. The rock in the earth's crust is like the 4. _____. It will bend for a while, but when pressure inside the 5. _____ is strong enough, the rock breaks apart. This sudden break causes the earth's 6. _____ to shake.

The vibrations from an earthquake are 7. _____ seismic waves. Seismic waves move outward from the center just as 8. _____ caused by a rock thrown in a pond move outward from the rock. Scientists use an instrument called a seismograph to record and measure 9. _____ waves.

Most 10. _____ occur in just two areas of the world. The Ring of Fire circles the Pacific Ocean. The Alptide Belt runs from southern Europe to Asia.

1. air ocean ground	2. he she it	3. stick pressure earth	4. air pressure stick	5. stick earth trees
6. crust atmosphere core	7. never called sometimes	8. waves seismic earthquake	9. water crust seismic	10. crust oceans earthquakes

Name _____

Mount Everest Maze

Mount Everest is the highest mountain in the world. Its summit is more than 5½ miles above sea level. Mount Everest is part of the Himalaya range in Asia. The first climbers to reach its peak were Sir Edmund Hillary and Tenzing Norgay. They reached the summit on May 29, 1953.

Draw a line to show the climbers the way from their base camp to the summit.

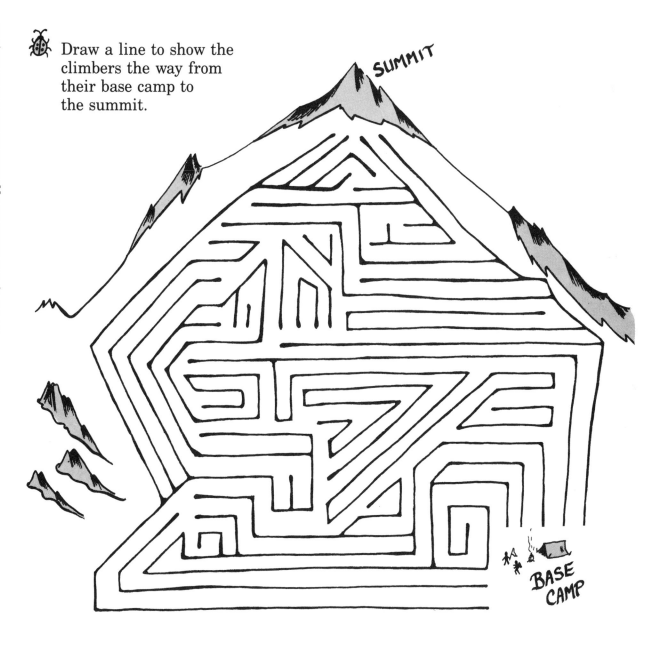

Name _____

How High?

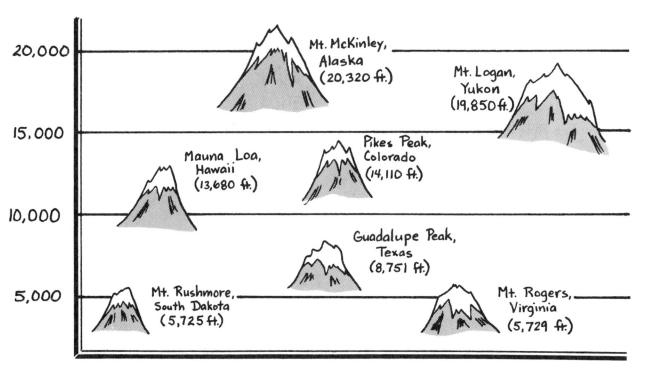

Use the graph to help you answer the questions.

1. How tall is the tallest mountain listed? _____

2. Where would you find the shortest mountain listed on the graph? _____

3. Which two mountains are more than 15,000 feet high? _____ _____

4. How tall is Mauna Loa? _____

5. Which mountain is taller than Mauna Loa and shorter than Mt. Logan? _____

6. How many mountains are less than 15,000 feet high? _____

BONUS: Which mountain is not part of the United States?

_____

Name _____

Geology Quick Check

 Use the word box to help you complete the sentences.

metal	core	fossils	glacier
crust	gravity	sphere	mantle

1. The earth is shaped like a flattened _____.

2. Magnets attract certain kinds of _____.

3. _____ are ancient prints in rock.

4. We live on the earth's _____.

5. _____ pulls everything to the earth's center.

6. The earth's _____ is made of molten rock.

7. A _____ is like a river of ice.

 Write "Yes" for true, and write "No" for not true.

8. _____ Folded mountains are caused by sideways pressure folding the earth's crust.

9. _____ Geysers shoot lava and steam in the air.

10. _____ Radiocarbon dating can tell how old a dinosaur bone is.

11. _____ The atmosphere surrounds our earth.

12. _____ Igneous rock is formed from sediment.

13. _____ Eons are short periods in Earth's history.

14. _____ Seismic waves move out from the center of an earthquake.

15. _____ Lava and ash force up to form volcanoes and volcanic mountains.

Handwriting—Weather

Does your umbrella always leak that way?

precipitation _____

_____

water vapor _____

_____

breeze _____

_____

gale _____

_____

lightning _____

_____

thunder _____

_____

hurricane _____

_____

tornado _____

_____

wind _____

_____

clouds _____

No... only when it rains!

_____

Name _____

What Makes Weather?

As you read this story, circle the correct word in each numbered box at the bottom of this sheet.

The sun gives the earth heat, light, and power. On warm summer 1. _____ the sun shines straight down on you for about 15 hours each day. On 2. _____ winter days the slanted rays of sunlight shine and warm you for about 9 3. _____ a day.

The sun is not the 4. _____ thing that helps to make weather. Air helps to make 5. _____, too. There is air all around the earth. Some say that the 6. _____ is "wrapped in a blanket" of air. When air is warmed by the sun, the air rises. As it rises, cooler air comes in underneath. We call this moving air wind and wind 7. _____ an important part of weather.

It takes 8. _____ than sunshine and air to make weather. Water is important, too. Water comes 9. _____ oceans, lakes, rivers, ponds, and even puddles. When water is warmed by the 10. _____, it becomes part of the air. This is evaporation. Water that has evaporated into the air forms clouds. Clouds make rain, hail, and snow.

1. years minutes days	2. cool hot warm	3. hours years days	4. some only most	5. sun nights weather
6. weather sky earth	7. are is were	8. only more just	9. from away around	10. moon stars sun

Name _____

All About Hurricanes and Tornadoes

 **Ready:**

enormous
tropical
equator
hurricane
homeless
recent
spiral
funnel
zigzag
forecaster

1. The _____ is an imaginary line around the earth's center.

2. Someone who has no place to live is _____.

3. "Tunnel" rhymes with _____.

4. If something is very, very large, it is _____.

5. If something is _____, it didn't happen very long ago.

6. A _____ predicts the weather.

© 1987 by The Center for Applied Research in Education, Inc.

 Set:

Hurricanes and tornadoes are dangerous storms. They create enormous waves that flood the land. Their winds are strong enough to destroy buildings and pull trees up by their roots.

Hurricanes begin over tropical ocean waters near the equator. The air above the water is heated by the sun and twists upward into a spiral. The calm air inside the spiral is called the eye of the hurricane. A hurricane's eye may be more than 15 miles across. The wind, rain, and clouds that circle the eye can be more than 600 miles across.

Name _____

One of the strongest hurricanes in recent times happened in 1935 in Tampa, Florida. The winds blew over 200 miles per hour. A huge 15-foot wall of water swept over the land. More than 400 people were killed and thousands were left homeless. Today forecasters can predict the path of a hurricane and warn the people in its way.

Tornadoes are much like hurricanes except they begin over land. Tornadoes are also called twisters or cyclones. The hollow center of a tornado is like a huge funnel that zigzags across the ground. Like a giant vacuum cleaner, the funnel sucks up things in its path. Scientists cannot predict exactly where a tornado may strike. They alert people with a "tornado watch."

 Go:

1. Hurricanes usually begin over (sky, land, water).

2. The calm air in the hurricane's center is called the _____ of the hurricane.

3. Forecasters can predict the path of a _____ but not the path of a _____.

4. The winds, rain, and clouds of a hurricane can be (15, 600, 1,000) miles across.

5. Tornadoes are also called twisters. (Yes, No)

6. In the 1935 hurricane, how many people died? _____

Name _____

More Than Just Water

As you read this story, circle the correct word in each numbered box at the bottom of this sheet.

When water evaporates into the air, it becomes water vapor. If the air cools, the 1. _____ vapor condenses and forms clouds 2. _____ with tiny water droplets. As more water condenses, the water droplets come 3. _____ and form larger drops. When these drops become too 4. _____ to stay in the air, they fall to the ground as rain.

If water drops 5. _____ through very cold air they freeze and 6. _____ sleet. Hail is another kind of 7. _____ rain. Hail is formed when water droplets are blown up by the wind to freeze 8. _____ and again. This repeated freezing forms layers of ice in the hail that you can see if you slice a large hailstone in half.

Snowflakes are not frozen raindrops. Snowflakes are 9. _____ by water vapor freezing before it can change into rain. Instead, the 10. _____ vapor quickly freezes into six-pointed ice crystals that fall as snow.

1. air water rain	2. under upper filled	3. from through together	4. heavy old light	5. fall back jump
6. become fall through	7. air water frozen	8. never again always	9. seen formed melted	10. snow rain water

Name _____

Thunder and Lightning

As you read this story, circle the correct word in each numbered box at the bottom of this sheet.

Almost everyone in North America has experienced thunderstorms. People living in the west have only a few 1. _____ each year. People on the east coast may see over one hundred of these storms each 2. _____.

Thunderstorms usually happen on summer afternoons. Huge, dark clouds 3. _____ thunderheads form as hot air quickly rises to meet higher cool 4. _____. Sometimes ice crystals form. These 5. _____ crystals are called hail.

Thunder is caused when air is 6. _____ heated by lightning. The roaring rumble of the 7. _____ across the sky is really echoing waves of sound.

You can tell about 8. _____ close the lightning is by counting the seconds between seeing lightning and 9. _____ thunder. Sound travels about 1 mile in 5 seconds. Ten seconds between 10. _____ and thunder means it is about 2 miles away.

1. snow hurricanes thunderstorms	2. year week day	3. called not even	4. dirt water air	5. black hot ice
6. not quickly most	7. lightning thunder rains	8. what how when	9. seeing hearing touching	10. lightning thunder clouds

Name _____

The Water Cycle

Water covers three quarters of our planet. Every living thing is part water. Water is part of a tree, a puppy, a whale, and even you.

Long ago people thought oceans flowed under the ground and back to the mountains. We know that this is not true, but water does go from the oceans to the mountains.

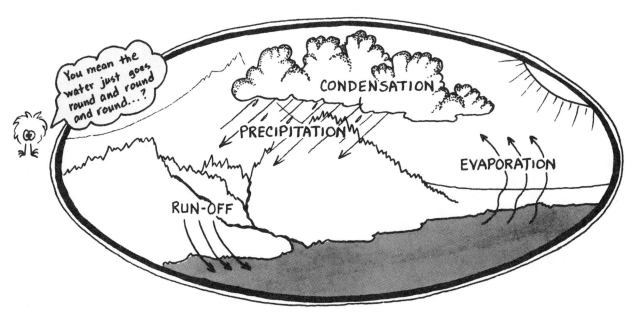

Water moves in a continuous cycle. The Sun's heat changes water into vapor. This is called evaporation. Ocean water evaporates and moves over the land. The moisture collects and forms clouds. As the clouds move farther inland, they rise to where the atmosphere is cooler. The cooler air causes condensation of water droplets. The condensed moisture falls as precipitation. We call it rain or snow.

Some water that falls to earth makes puddles. These evaporate and return to the atmosphere. Some water travels as run-off down streams and rivers back to the oceans. Water absorbed by plants returns to the air through a special process called transpiration.

The Earth's water supply moves, but the amount of water never changes. We have no more or less water now than when dinosaurs walked the Earth 3½ billion years ago. Water is in constant motion among the oceans, land, and atmosphere.

Name _____

 Use these words to help you complete each sentence.

evaporation		precipitation		condensation
ocean	vapor	atmosphere	amount	sun
three	cloud	run-off	water	living

1. Water is changed to vapor by heat from the _____.

2. _____ quarters of the Earth is covered by water.

3. Rain and snow are types of _____.

4. The Earth's water moves, but the _____always stays the same.

5. _____ is water traveling down rivers and streams back to the oceans.

6. Evaporation is heat changing water into _____.

7. Cooler air causes _____of water droplets.

8. Water is part of every _____thing.

Name _____

All About Clouds

 **Ready:**

| predict |
| cumulus |
| stratus |
| hazy |
| drizzly |
| cirrus |
| feathery |
| wispy |
| formation |
| nimbus |

1. A word that rhymes with "daisy" is _____.

2. _____ means the same as "forecast."

3. On a _____ day very light rain or mist falls.

4. A _____ cloud is a rainstorm cloud.

5. Another word for feathery is _____.

 Set:

Over one hundred years ago, Luke Howard, an English scientist, studied the clouds. He watched for many days and discovered four main types of clouds. He gave the types of clouds names that came from ancient Latin words.

Clouds that are closest to the earth he called cumulus clouds. Cumulus in Latin means "heap" or "pile." Thick cumulus clouds are flat on the bottom and appear to be piled high on top like a fluffy dome.

Howard called the thin flat clouds he saw stratus clouds. Stratus is a Latin word that means "spread out." Stratus clouds are always flat on the bottom and on the top. These clouds cover hundreds of miles on hazy, drizzly days when there is little sunlight.

Name _____

The third kind of clouds, cirrus clouds, got their name from the Latin word for "curl." These feathery clouds are like wispy curls of white hair. Cirrus are the highest clouds. They can be 10 miles above the earth. Although they appear to travel slowly, they move 100 to 200 miles per hour!

Nimbus clouds are the fourth kind of cloud formation. Nimbus means "rainstorm" in Latin. These clouds make thunderstorms and hail. Thunderheads develop from cumulo-nimbus clouds.

Look at the clouds as Luke Howard did. Try to see what kind they are. The clouds may even help you predict the weather.

 Go:

1. Who gave the four groups of clouds their Latin names? _____ _____

2. _____ clouds are flat on the bottom and fluffy on top.

3. Thin, flat, spread-out clouds are _____clouds.

4. Thin, wispy clouds that are highest in the sky are called _____clouds.

5. Nimbus clouds are rainstorm clouds. (Yes, No)

6. What word from the last paragraph means "to foretell the future?" _____

Name _____

Weather or Climate?

Climate is the average or usual weather patterns of an area. Like weather, the elements of climate are temperature, moisture, precipitation, wind, and air pressure.

The important difference between weather and climate is time. Weather is about a certain time. Climate is about long-range conditions. If you say that it rained on your birthday you are talking about weather. If you say that the Rockies have cold, snowy winters you are talking about climate.

Generally, climates are warmer as you move toward the equator and colder near the poles. Altitude also affects climate. The higher you go above sea level, the cooler the climate. That is why very high mountains may have snow caps all year around.

Climates are often described by the seasons. A place may have hot, dry summers and cold winters. Another place may have heavy rains in the spring and fall. Whatever the climate is, it is an average of many years weather and describes the usual weather patterns.

Using the boxes, draw a picture for each season. In your pictures show the average or usual weather where you live. Then complete the sentences to describe your seasons and the climate in your area.

1. Where I live winter is _____

_____

2. Where I live summer is _____

_____

3. Where I live autumn is _____

_____

4. Where I live spring is _____

_____

5. Where I live the climate is _____

_____

_____

Name _____

Picture Boxes for "Weather or Climate?"

Winter	Spring
Summer	Autumn

Lost in the Clouds

Help the pilot find a way through the storm to the hangar.

Name _____

Weather Word Search

Look for each of these words in the word search. The words can be found either across or down.

BAROMETER   HYGROMETER

THERMOMETER   RAIN GAUGE

METEOROLOGIST   FORECAST

ANEMOMETER   PRECIPITATION

RAINFALL   TEMPERATURE

AIR PRESSURE

HUMIDITY

Name _____

Forecasting Tools

Meteorologists keep track of changes in the weather and gather information using special instruments. You have probably seen one of these special tools, a thermometer, many times. A thermometer measures the air temperature.

Two instruments help meteorologists measure the wind. A wind vane shows the wind's direction. An anemometer or wind gauge measures the speed of the wind. An anemometer is made of four cups that spin around as the wind blows.

Changes in air pressure usually mean changes in the weather. Meteorologists measure air pressure with a barometer.

A hygrometer measures the amount of moisture or water vapor in the air. The measurement is usually called humidity. For example, a meteorologist might say the humidity is 10 percent. This means the air is very dry.

Clouds are very important in forecasting. Special cameras on weather satellites help meteorologists predict the weather. Pictures transmitted from miles above the earth show cloud patterns over a very large area.

Meteorologists measure rainfall in a rain gauge. Like a special measuring cup, the rain gauge catches the falling rain and shows the number of inches collected.

Below each instrument, name it and tell what it measures. One is done for you.

© 1987 by The Center for Applied Research in Education, Inc.

Name: Barometer

Measures: Air Pressure

Name: _____ (1)

Measures: _____ (2)

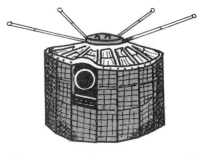

Name: _____ (3)

Measures: _____ (4)

Name: _____ (5)

Measures: _____ (6)

Name: _____ (7)

Measures: _____ (8)

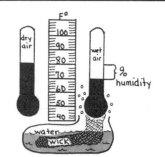

Name: _____ (9)

Measures: _____ (10)

Name _____

Mapping the Weather

A weather map can tell you many things about the weather in many different places. Most newspapers print a weather map each day. These maps are made by the United States Weather Bureau. If you know how to read a weather map, you can forecast the weather.

Symbols are used on weather maps to tell about sky conditions, wind speed, and direction of the wind. Numbers are used to tell the temperature at the time the map was made.

This chart shows the symbols for sky conditions:

An arrow attached to the sky condition symbol tells the wind speed. Each long line on the arrow means 10 mph. Each short line means 5 mph. This symbol 〇⋙ tells us that the sky is partly cloudy and the wind speed is 35 mph.

The weather symbol also tells the direction of the wind. The arrow points the wind direction just like the arrow of a compass. This symbol ⋙Ⓡ tells us that it is raining and the wind is blowing from the west at 25 mph.

 Use the map to help you answer these questions.

1. What is the sky condition in San Francisco today? _____

2. Would it be a good day for swimming in Seattle? _____Why? _____

3. What is the wind direction in Atlanta? _____

4. Will you need an umbrella in Miami? _____

5. Which city has the highest temperature reading? _____

6. Which city is cloudy? _____

7. Where would you go for a suntan? _____

8. Which city is partly cloudy with a northwest wind blowing 25 mph? _____

9. Where would a raincoat be the most useful? _____

Name _____

Weather Map

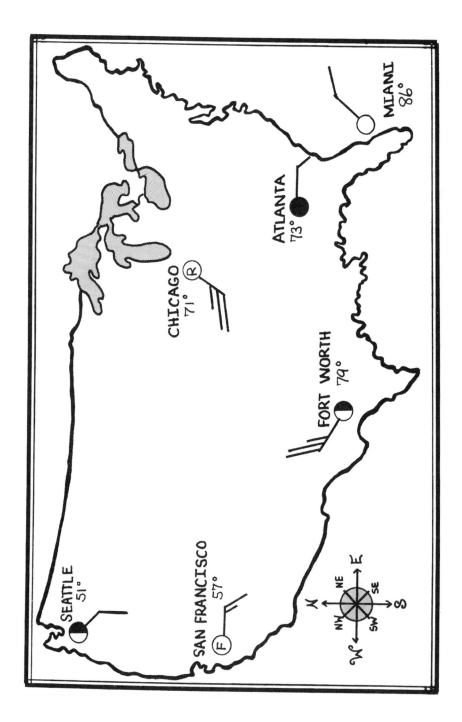

Name _____

Breeze or Gale?

In 1805, an admiral in the British navy, named Sir Francis Beaufort, made up a system for measuring wind speeds. The Beaufort Scale gave names, numbers, and symbols to different wind speeds. Beaufort first made his scale to help sailing ships. Today his scale helps to chart winds on land and sea.

Read each statement and use the Beaufort Scale to help you answer the questions.

While listening to the radio, you hear the announcer say that the wind is blowing at 15 mph.

1. What is the symbol for this wind? _____

2. What would you see swaying outside? _____

3. What is the name given to this wind speed? _____

You look out your window one morning and see large branches blowing on the trees.

4. How fast is the wind blowing? _____

5. What is the Beaufort number for this wind speed? _____

6. What is the symbol for this wind?_____

On the newspaper weather map you find this symbol ⊙— near your city.

7. What is the name given to this wind speed? _____

8. How fast is the wind blowing? _____

9. Where does smoke from your chimney go? _____

The Beaufort Scale
for "Breeze or Gale?"

Beaufort Number	Symbol	Name	MPH	Effects of the Wind
0	○—	Calm	0	Smoke rises straight up
1	○⁄	Light Air	1-3	Smoke drifts
2	○⁄	Light Breeze	4-7	Weather vanes move
3	○⁄⁄	Gentle Breeze	8-12	Leaves and twigs blow
4	○⁄⁄	Moderate Breeze	13-18	Small branches move on trees
5	○⁄⁄⁄	Fresh Breeze	19-24	Small trees sway
6	○⁄⁄⁄	Strong Breeze	25-31	Larger branches move on trees
7	○⁄⁄⁄	Moderate Gale	32-38	Whole trees move
8	○⁄⁄⁄⁄	Fresh Gale	39-46	Twigs on trees break
9	○⁄⁄⁄⁄	Strong Gale	47-54	Slight building damage
10	○⁄⁄⁄⁄	Whole Gale	55-63	Trees uprooted - more bldg. dam.
11	○⁄⁄⁄⁄⁄	Storm	64-72	Widespread damage on land
12	○⁄⁄⁄⁄⁄	Hurricane	73+	Violent destruction on land

Name _____

All About Weather Rhymes

 Ready:

simple
rhymes
instruments
forecast
predict
agree
actually
facing
crackling
static

1. Two words that mean "to foretell the future" are _____

   and _____.

2. People who share the same opinion _____ about something.

3. _____ are mechanical tools.

4. Crack is the base word in the word _____.

5. If something is easy to learn and remember it is _____.

 Set:

"Rain, rain go away. Come again another day…" You probably know this short simple rhyme about the weather. There are many such rhymes, but have you ever wondered where they came from?

Most of these rhymes are very, very old. They were first said before people had instruments or maps to help forecast the weather. They were said before there were radios, televisions, and newspapers to give people weather reports. Often the rhymes were made up by farmers from weather signs they saw in nature.

Not all weather rhymes are true, but some did help to predict changes in the weather. See if you agree. "A ring around the sun or moon, brings rain or snow upon us soon." The ring you see is actually ice crystals in the clouds high in the sky. These crystals make the ring appear.

"Cow with its tail to the west, makes the weather best." Have you ever seen cows standing in a field facing the same way? Cows like to stand with their tails to the wind. In this rhyme, winds from the west mean good weather ahead.

Most of these weather rhymes are at least partly true. Think about the things you see in nature. Perhaps you can make up a weather rhyme, too.

 Go:

1. Words that rhyme have the same (beginning, middle, ending) sound.

2. Weather forecasters use _____ and maps to help predict the weather.

3. _____ crystals cause a ring around the sun or moon.

4. Cows like to stand facing the wind. (Yes, No)

5. Weather rhymes were often made up by _____ from the weather signs they saw in nature.

6. All weather rhymes are true. (Yes, No)

Name _____

All About Weather Myths

 Ready:

legend
custom
myth
hibernation
shadow
common
swallows
calendar
mission
migrate

1. A _____ and a _____ are stories that have been told many times.

2. _____ rhymes with "follows."

3. Birds _____ from one region to another.

4. _____ has four syllables.

5. Something that is ordinary or usual could be called _____.

6. We can keep track of the days, months, and years with

   a _____.

 Set:

All of us have heard myths about the weather. One of the most common is the legend of Groundhog day. This custom was brought to America by people from Great Britain and Germany. According to their legend, the groundhog awakes from hibernation on February 2nd and sticks his head out of his den. If the sun is shining, the groundhog sees his shadow and crawls back into his hole. This is supposed to mean six more weeks of winter. If February 2nd is cloudy, the groundhog does not see his shadow and he stays outside. This is supposed to mean spring will come soon. This myth is so common that you often see Groundhog Day printed on many calendars.

Another common myth about the beginning of spring is the legend of the Capistrano swallows. San Juan Capistrano is a small town near Los Angeles in California. It was first settled as a mission in 1776.

Each year the swallows migrate from Capistrano around October 23rd. They return each spring on March 19th. Many people wait for the swallows as a sign that spring is coming.

 Go:

1. A story retold from one person to another is a (song, legend, book).

2. The _____ is a small animal that legend says can foretell the end of winter.

3. If the groundhog sees his shadow spring is still (6, 12, 10) weeks away.

4. In what state would you find San Juan Capistrano? _____

5. Swallows leave Capistrano in the spring. (Yes, No)

6. What word in the last paragraph means "to move from one region to another"?

_____

Name _____

Grade the Forecaster

 Choose one television or radio forecaster to grade for 5 days. On the report card below, record each day's forecast. Later record what the real weather was like. Then use a symbol to show how close the forecast was to the real weather for each day.

 Report Card

Forecaster's Name _____

DATE	FORECAST	REAL WEATHER	GRADE

Symbols: ☺ right   😐 close   ☹ not close   😠 wrong

 Did your forecaster do a good job? _____

Why or why not? _____

_____

Name _____

A "Hairy" Hygrometer

You can make a hygrometer to measure humidity. You will need an index card, a human hair about 9 inches long, an 8 x 11 inch piece of cardboard, a thumb tack, tape, a ruler, and scissors.

First draw a 6-inch arrow on the index card. Cut out the arrow. Next, tape one end of the hair near the top of the cardboard. Tape the loose end of the hair to the back of the arrow's pointed end. Carefully stretch the hair to full length. Attach the blunt end of the arrow with the tack.

"Set" your hygrometer by marking where the arrow points on a very damp day and a dry day.

 In the circles, number the steps in the correct order.

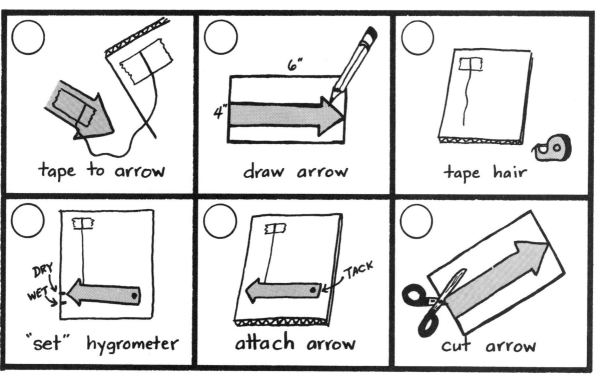

tape to arrow

draw arrow

tape hair

"set" hygrometer

attach arrow

cut arrow

Highs and Lows

This chart from an evening newspaper shows the high and low temperatures for eight cities. In the spaces below, subtract to find the temperature difference for each of the cities.

NATIONAL TEMPERATURES		
City	High	Low
Anchorage	29°	24°
Chicago	63°	43°
Denver	71°	47°
Houston	78°	68°
Los Angeles	81°	50°
Miami	83°	79°
New York	62°	47°
Washington	57°	55°

1. Anchorage $\begin{array}{r} 29° \\ -24° \\ \hline °\end{array}$	2. Chicago	3. Denver	4. Houston
5. Los Angeles	6. Miami	7. New York	8. Washington

Is there a National Weather chart in your newspaper?

BONUS: Look at the high temperatures on the chart. Begin with the warmest and list the cities in order by their high temperature. _____

_____

_____

Name _____

Weather Quick Check

 Use the word box to help you complete the sentences.

thunder	precipitation	wind	climate
evaporates	nimbus	tornadoes	cycle

1. Rain and snow are kinds of _____.

2. Water moves from land to sea to air and back again in the water _____.

3. Hurricanes and _____ are spiraling or twisting storms.

4. When lightning quickly heats the air it causes _____.

5. _____ is an average of many years of weather.

6. When water _____ it becomes water vapor.

 Write "Yes" for true and "No" for not true.

7. _____ "Forecast" means to predict future events.

8. _____ The Beaufort Scale measures wind speeds.

9. _____ Weather maps only give temperatures for a certain place.

10. _____ Barometers measure the air temperature.

11. _____ Partly cloudy is a sky condition.

12. _____ A 25-mph wind is a light breeze.

13. _____ Groundhogs and swallows can predict the weather.

Name _____

  # Handwriting—Planets

Sun _____

_____

Mercury _____

_____

Venus _____

_____

Earth _____

_____

Mars _____

_____

Jupiter _____

_____

Saturn _____

_____

Uranus _____

_____

Neptune _____

_____

Pluto _____

_____

Name _____

The Sun

As you read this story, circle the correct word in each numbered box at the bottom of this sheet.

Our sun is a star, like the billions of our stars. It seems bigger and brighter to us

1. _____ it is much closer than the other stars. Even so, the sun is 93 million

2. _____ from Earth! Scientists believe the 3. _____ was formed from a cloud of

spinning gas and dust. As the cloud spun 4. _____, it compacted to form our sun.

The sun is the 5. _____ member of the solar system. 6. _____ diameter is 865

thousand miles. About one million earths 7. _____ fit inside of the sun. The surface of

the 8. _____ is like a sea of white-hot gas. Its temperature is about 11,000 degrees

Fahrenheit. A hot day here on earth is only about 98 degrees!

The earth would be very 9. _____ without the sun's heat and light. Plants turn
the sun's energy into food for animals—even you. Without the sun, the earth would be

cold, 10. _____, and lifeless.

The sun's light takes 8½ minutes to reach the earth.

1. because	2. feet	3. moon	4. faster	5. coldest
but	yards	sun	over	smallest
either	miles	clouds	fell	largest
6. Her	7. don't	8. earth	9. different	10. hot
His	were	sun	same	dark
Its	could	moon	hot	dry

Name _____

Phases of the Moon

The shape of the moon does not change. It does look different to us at different times each month. Sometimes the moon looks round and full. Other times it appears like a thin curve. These different ways the moon looks are called "phases."

The first phase of the moon is the "new moon." The moon is between the sun and the earth so we see no moon at all. After a few nights, a crescent-shaped part of the moon can be seen. Each night, a little more of the lighted moon shows in the sky. During this time, we say the moon is "waxing." Waxing means to increase or grow larger.

At the end of the two weeks, the moon is round and full. Now the moon and sun are on opposite sides of the earth. The moon continues to revolve around the earth. Each night the light reflection of the moon grows smaller. We now say the moon is "waning." Waning means to decrease.

By the end of the third week, the moon again looks crescent-shaped. During the fourth week, it seems again to disappear. It is time for the cycle to begin again. The moon has made one revolution around the earth. One month has passed and a new month is about to begin.

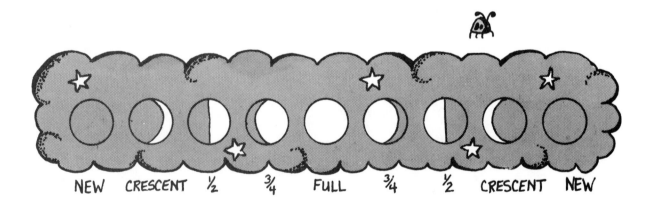

NEW   CRESCENT   ½   ¾   FULL   ¾   ½   CRESCENT   NEW

Name _____

Write the number of each moon next to its description:

1.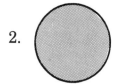

          _____ ☆ When the moon and the sun are on opposite sides of the earth, the moon is full.

2.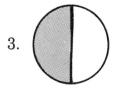

          _____ ☆ As the moon waxes toward a full moon, we see ¾ of its lighted side.

3.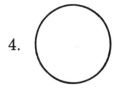

          _____ ☆ On the night of a new moon, the dark side of the moon is towards the earth.

4.

          _____ ☆ The moon wanes toward a new moon and shows only a lighted crescent moon.

5.

          _____ ☆ When we see half light and half dark, the moon is called a half moon.

Have you ever heard someone say "once in a blue moon"? It takes 28 days for the moon to complete one revolution. Because most calendar months have 30 or 31 days, sometimes the moon is full twice in one month. A "blue moon" is the second full moon in one month. It doesn't happen often. Something "once in a blue moon" is very rare indeed.

Name _____

Did you know there are 30,000 craters on the moon?

A Natural Satellite

As you read this story, circle the correct word in each numbered box at the bottom of this sheet.

The moon is our closest neighbor in space. It is about 240,000 miles from the earth. It is much 1. _____ than the earth and has only ⅙ of Earth's gravity. If you weigh 60 2. _____ here, you would weigh only 10 pounds on the moon.

The moon has no 3. _____ of its own. The moonlight we see is actually reflected sunlight. There is no air or 4. _____ on the moon. Living things need air and water so there is no life on the 5. _____.

The full moon looks like a giant 6. _____ of rock. The lighter parts are rough, rocky mountains with valleys 7. _____ craters. The darker surface areas are "seas." These moon seas contain no water. They 8. _____ like smooth, dust-covered deserts.

The moon is our earth's natural satellite. It orbits 9. _____ the earth about every 28 days. As the moon circles the 10. _____, the earth's shadow falls on the moon. This causes the phases of the moon.

1. larger darker smaller	2. ounces pounds tons	3. light dirt crater	4. dust mountain water	5. moon earth ocean
6. cube ball hill	7. not were called	8. is was are	9. under around over	10. sun earth moon

Name _____

Twinkle, Twinkle

As you read this story, circle the correct word in each numbered box at the bottom of this sheet.

Stars are spheres of glowing, hot gas that shine brightly in the night sky. The sun is our closest 1. _____. It is an average size star. Some are smaller 2. _____ our moon. Others are thousands of times 3. _____ than our sun. The biggest 4. _____ are "supergiants." The smallest stars are "neutron stars."

Stars 5. _____ mostly hydrogen, which burns and gives off energy. Starlight is the energy we see. We 6. _____ starlight through our atmosphere. Looking through the 7. _____ is much like looking through water. Stars don't twinkle. The atmosphere just makes 8. _____ look as if they do!

In ancient times, people looked at the stars and 9. _____ drawings of what they saw. When they connected the 10. _____ with lines, they created pictures of folk heroes, gods, and animals. On a clear night, see how many of these constellations you can find. Use a star book or chart to help you.

With just your eyes, you can see over 2000 stars!

1. moon planet star	2. than or under	3. darker larger stronger	4. suns stars moons	5. are is am
6. hear touch see	7. water atmosphere stars	8. they them this	9. bought were made	10. stars planets moons

Name _____

All About an Eclipse

 **Ready:**

| ancient |
| eclipse |
| evil |
| heavenly |
| solar |
| lunar |
| directly |
| partial |
| visible |
| shadow |

1. A word that means the opposite of "good" is _____.

2. Something you can see is said to be _____.

3. _____ has the same "oo" sound as "moon."

4. The root word in _____ is "part."

5. _____ means "having to do with the sun."

6. _____ means "very old."

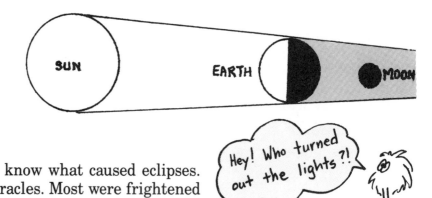

 Set:

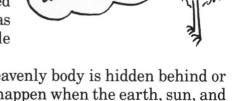

Ancient people did not know what caused eclipses. Some thought they were miracles. Most were frightened by them. In China, people once believed an eclipse was caused by an evil dragon eating up the sun. The people would make loud noises to scare the dragon away.

Today, we know that an eclipse occurs when one heavenly body is hidden behind or in the shadow of another. Eclipses of our sun and moon happen when the earth, sun, and moon move into a straight line. When only part of the sun or moon is hidden, we have a partial eclipse. All of the sun or moon is hidden in a total eclipse.

Name ————————————————

An eclipse of the sun is a solar eclipse. This happens when the moon passes directly between the sun and the earth. As the moon approaches a straight line with the sun, the sky darkens. In minutes, the sun is hidden. As the moon continues across the sky, the day becomes bright again. Solar eclipses happen only about once every 18 years and last only about 7 minutes!

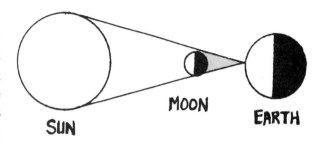

A lunar eclipse is an eclipse of the moon. They are much more common than solar eclipses. There are usually one or two visible lunar eclipses each year. A lunar eclipse may last for 90 minutes or more.

 Go:

1. In Ancient China, people believed a ————————————— was eating the sun during an eclipse.

2. Things having to do with the sun and its planets are (lunar, solar, partial).

3. A ————————————————————————— eclipse can last 90 minutes or more.

4. About how often do solar eclipses happen? —————————————————————————

5. Eclipses happen when the —————————————, —————————————, and ————————————————————————————— are in a straight line.

6. A solar eclipse lasts only about (2, 7, 30) minutes.

Name ———————————

Family of Planets

A planet is a celestial body that moves in an orbit around a star. Our earth is a planet. It moves around the sun. There are nine planets in our solar system. All of them travel around our sun.

The planet closest to the sun is Mercury. Then comes Venus. Next, about 26 million miles from Venus, is our earth. Mercury and Venus are hotter planets than Earth because they are closer to the sun. The other planets, Mars, Jupiter, Saturn, Uranus, Neptune, and Pluto, are farther from the sun. They are much colder than Earth.

Some planets are larger than Earth. Some planets are smaller. Mercury, Venus, Earth, Mars, and Pluto are "small planets." They are made mostly of rock. Large planets, called "giant planets," are mostly hot liquid and gases. Jupiter, Saturn, Uranus, and Neptune are giant planets.

You know that our earth has one moon. Did you also know that some planets have more than one moon? A moon is a natural satellite traveling in an orbit around a planet. Mars has two moons. Uranus has five moons. Jupiter, the largest planet, has at least fifteen moons!

Here is a picture of our solar system. On the lines below the picture, write the names of the planets. Earth is done for you. HINT: Write one letter for each space.

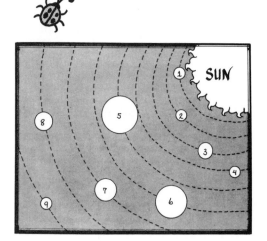

1. ___ ___ ___ ___ ___ ___ ___

2. ___ ___ ___ ___ ___

3. E A R T H

4. ___ ___ ___ ___

5. ___ ___ ___ ___ ___ ___ ___

6. ___ ___ ___ ___ ___ ___

7. ___ ___ ___ ___ ___ ___

8. ___ ___ ___ ___ ___ ___ ___

9. ___ ___ ___ ___ ___

If the statement is true, write "Yes." If the statement is not true, write "No":

10. _____ All planets travel in an orbit.

11. _____ Planets are all about the same size.

12. _____ Planets closest to the sun are very cold.

13. _____ Many planets have more than one moon.

14. _____ The small planets are mostly hot liquid.

15. _____ Venus is about 26 miles away from Earth.

16. _____ Our solar system has nine planets.

"Celestial" means "of the sky."

Name _____

All About Shooting Stars

 **Ready:**

materials
comet
famous
appeared
atmosphere
streak
meteor
occasional
survives
crater

1. Something that is well known to many people is _____.

2. _____ has the same "i" sound as "like."

3. A _____ is a hole made by a lump of rock hitting the earth.

4. _____ rhymes with "week."

5. The air surrounding our earth is its _____.

6. Another word for "sometimes" is _____.

 Set:

We usually think of the space between the sun, moon, and planets as being empty. Actually, it is not. Our solar system is full of rocks, clouds of dust, and frozen gases. Sometimes we see these materials in the sky as comets or meteors.

Comets are masses of dust and frozen gases. Some scientists say they are like "dirty snowballs" in space. Comets are rare. Most are named for the first person to discover them. It passes near the earth every 76 years. Long ago, people were afraid of comets. When Halley's Comet appeared in 1910 people even bought "comet pills" to protect them from the comet's harm.

We don't see comets very often, but we can see meteors nearly every night. These shooting stars are not stars at all. They are lumps of rock and metal burning up in our atmosphere. We see them as glowing streaks in the night sky. Usually meteors burn up completely long before reaching the earth. Occasionally, a meteor survives and crashes to the ground. A large meteor may cause a hole or crater when it strikes the earth. The largest of these craters is in Arizona. It measures 4,150 feet across and 575 feet deep. The largest meteor ever found on earth is now in New York's American Museum of Natural History. It weighs 30 tons!

On a clear night you may see 10 to 20 meteors every hour.

 Go:

1. The space between the earth, sun, and moon is empty. (No, Yes)

2. Scientists say comets are like _____ snowballs in space.

3. We see meteors (more, less, just as) often as we see comets.

4. Shooting stars are not really stars at all. (No, Yes)

5. The hole left by a large meteor striking the earth is a _____.

Name _____

The Sky Dragon

Connect the dots to see "Draco—The Sky Dragon"

This constellation is best seen in July when the "Big Dipper" is sloping through the west.

"Draco" is between the handle of the "Big Dipper" and the bowl of the "Little Dipper."

Ancient people believed the stars were golden apples guarded by the dragon. "Falling stars" were golden apples dropping from the sky.

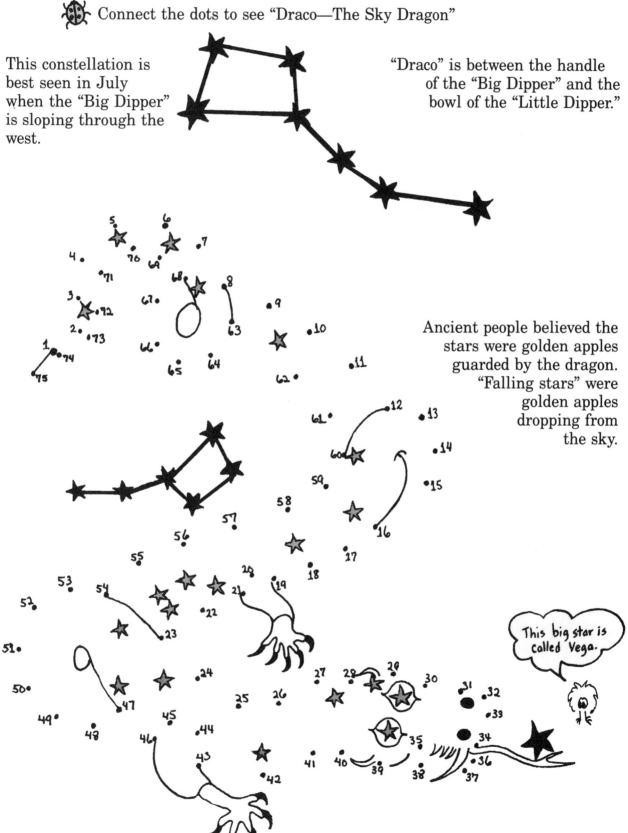

This big star is called Vega.

Name _____

SPACE
SPUTNIK
TELESCOPE

Space Word Search

Look for each of these words in the word search. The words can be found either across or down.

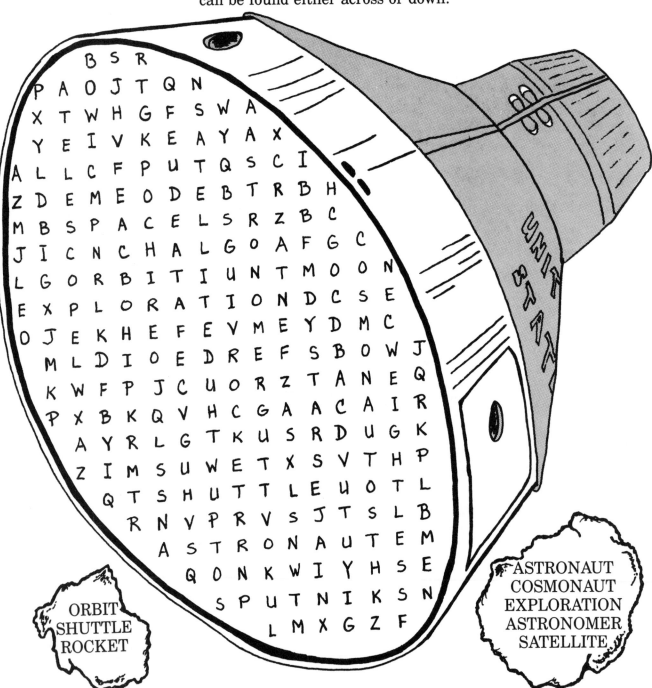

```
    B S R
  P A O J T Q N
X T W H G F S W A
Y E I V K E A Y A X
A L L C F P U T Q S C I
Z D E M E O D E B T R B H
M B S P A C E L S R Z B C
J I C N H A L G O A F G C
L G O R B I T I U N T M O O N
E X P L O R A T I O N D C S E
O J E K H E F E V M E Y D M C
M L D I O E D R E F S B O W J
K W F P J C U O R Z T A N E Q
P X B K Q V H C G A A C A I R
A Y R L G T K U S R D U G K
Z I M S U W E T X S V T H P
  Q T S H U T T L E U O T L
  R N V P R V S J T S L B
  A S T R O N A U T E M
  Q O N K W I Y H S E
  S P U T N I K S N
    L M X G Z F
```

ORBIT
SHUTTLE
ROCKET

ASTRONAUT
COSMONAUT
EXPLORATION
ASTRONOMER
SATELLITE

Name _____

All About Early Astronomers

 Ready:

orbit
motionless
severe
astronomer
gadget
lenses
reflected
punished
telescopes
satellite

1. A person who studies celestial bodies is an _____.

2. _____ means the opposite of "rewarded."

3. The moon is a _____ of the earth.

4. A word that means "still or not moving" is _____.

5. Something harsh or serious is _____.

 Set:

Long ago, people believed the earth was the center of everything. They thought that the sun, planets, and stars revolved in an orbit around a motionless Earth. No one was allowed to say this was not true. If they did, they were severely punished.

In 1543, a Polish astronomer named Nicolaus Copernicus wrote a book saying that the earth moved around the sun. He had no way to prove that he was right and few people believed him.

Then in 1608 a Dutch eyeglass maker named Hans Lippershey built a gadget made of lenses and a tube. The gadget made far away things appear closer. He called his invention a "magic tube." Today we call it a telescope.

Soon, Galileo Galilei, an Italian astronomer, heard about the "magic tube." He improved the lenses and built many telescopes. With them, he studied the moon, stars, and planets. Galileo discovered sunspots, satellites around Jupiter, and Saturn's rings. He found valleys and mountains on the moon and that the moon's light was reflected from the sun.

Galileo spoke and wrote about all the wonders he saw with his telescopes. For doing this, he was put into prison. He was made to promise that he would never again teach about the earth moving around the sun. Galileo was punished for being the first man to get a close-up view of space.

Go:

1. Long ago, people believed the (moon, earth, sun) was the center of everything.

2. Today, we call Lippershey's "magic tube" a _____.

3. Where was Galileo put for writing and teaching about what he saw? _____

4. Galileo and Copernicus believed the earth went around the _____.

5. Galileo discovered mountains on the moon. (Yes, No)

Name _____

Satellites

As you read this story, circle the correct word in each numbered box at the bottom of this sheet.

A satellite is an object that revolves around a planet. Some satellites weigh many tons. Others 1. _____ only a few pounds. Our moon is a natural satellite of 2. _____.

Satellites travel through 3. _____ in paths called orbits. An orbit can be like a circle with a planet as its center. Our moon moves 4. _____ the earth in a circular 5. _____. Most satellites have egg-shaped orbits.

A satellite stays in orbit because it travels 6. _____ fast for gravity to pull it down. The pull of 7. _____ is only strong enough to keep 8. _____ satellite from flying off into space.

Not all satellites are natural. Man-made satellites are launched 9. _____ space by rockets. These satellites help transmit radio 10. _____ television signals. They even help forecast our weather!

1. way	2. Mars	3. space	4. under	5. orbit
weigh	Earth	air	over	moon
weight	Pluto	water	around	center
6. not	7. gravity	8. them	9. into	10. but
much	magnets	those	under	not
too	glue	the	over	and

Name _____

Animal Astronauts

As you read this story, circle the correct word in each numbered box at the bottom of this sheet.

The world's first space traveler was a small black and white dog named Laika. In 1957, she 1. _____ the Russian satellite, Sputnik 2, into space. Laika had been trained to be calm and to sit 2. _____ still for many hours. During the flight, she 3. _____ strapped to a special seat. Instruments were attached to her 4. _____ to listen to her heart beat and to record her breathing. Cameras 5. _____ the capsule took pictures of Laika.

Dogs have not been the only 6. _____ to travel in space. Monkeys, chimpanzees, mice, rats, 7. _____ spiders are some of the creatures to have ridden in a 8. _____ capsule. These animals give scientists information about how space travel affects 9. _____ creatures.

Laika and other 10. _____ astronauts have made it possible for humans to travel safely into space.

"Sputnik" means "traveling companion" in Russian

1. rode lost kept	2. much many very	3. were is was	4. head body tail	5. inside under behind
6. animals people dogs	7. not but and	8. time space empty	9. old dead living	10. people animal satellite

Name _____

All About Footprints on the Moon

 Ready:

mankind
surface
astronaut
capsule
launch
gravity
orbit
lunar
rod
crew

1. A person who travels in space is an _____.

2. A _____ is like a thin straight stick.

3. _____ pulls objects toward a planet's center.

4. People working together are sometimes called a _____.

5. The outside of a planet's crust is its _____.

 Set:

"That's one small step for a man, one giant leap for mankind." Neil Armstrong said these words as he took man's first step onto the surface of the moon.

Neil Armstrong, Edwin Aldrin, and Michael Collins were the astronauts of Apollo 11. Only 3 were inside the space capsule, but 400,000 people worked to make their trip possible. The planning and building of Apollo 11 took nearly 10 years.

The Apollo 11 was launched from Cape Kennedy on July 16, 1969. The space capsule was in two parts. Together, they traveled away from Earth's gravity and into lunar orbit. The Command Module with Collins inside stayed in orbit. Armstrong and Aldrin landed the Lunar Module on the moon on July 20, 1969.

Name _____

While the astronauts were on the moon, they took pictures and scooped up rocks to bring back to Earth. They also put up a United States flag. Because the moon has no wind, the flag had to be held out by a stiff rod.

While Armstrong and Aldrin were on the moon, President Richard Nixon telephoned to congratulate them. His call was *really* long distance—238,000 miles!

The Apollo 11 astronauts left many footprints on the moon's surface. Because there is no rain or wind on the moon, the prints still look just as they did in 1969. The Apollo 11 crew also left behind a plaque. It reads, "We came in peace for all mankind."

The lunar module, "Eagle," was on the moon for 21 hours and 37 minutes.

Go:

1. The Apollo 11 space capsule had (1, 2, 3) parts.

2. All three astronauts walked on the moon. (Yes, No)

3. Tell two things the astronauts did while on the moon:

   a. _____

   b. _____

4. When did man first step on the moon? _____

5. Why are Neil Armstrong's footprints still on the moon after so many years? _____

   _____

6. Who telephoned the astronauts? _____

Name _____

Man in Space

Read about these historic events in man's exploration of space. Then follow the directions below.

▲ Sputniks 1 and 2 were launched in 1957. Laika was the first living creature in space.

▲ Both the United States and the USSR launched the first men into space in 1961.

▲ In 1962, John Glenn became the first American to orbit Earth.

▲ The USSR sent the first woman into space in 1963. She orbitted Earth 48 times.

▲ For the first time, astronauts left their spacecrafts to walk in space in 1965.

▲ The first soft landings on the moon were made by both the US and the USSR in 1966.

▲ United States astronaut Neil Armstrong made the first footprints on the moon in 1969.

▲ The space shuttle "Columbia" was launched in 1981. It was the first spacecraft to land like an airplane.

 Fill in the date for each event. Cut along the heavy lines. Glue the pictures in order to a paper strip to make a timeline.

Walk in Space
date:_____

U.S. Orbits Earth
date:_____

Soft Moon Landing
date:_____

Moon Footprints
date:_____

Space Shuttle
date:_____

Woman in Space
date:_____

Sputnik
date:_____

Men in Space
date:_____

Name _____

All About Mars

 **Ready:**

| century |
| rust |
| soil |
| surface |
| canyons |
| craters |
| channel |
| revolution |
| seasons |
| liquid |

1. _____ is a reddish brown color.

2. Winter, spring, summer, and fall are the _____ of the year.

3. One hundred years is called a _____.

4. _____ is another name for "dirt."

5. Water is a _____.

6. _____ means "a groove like a river's bed."

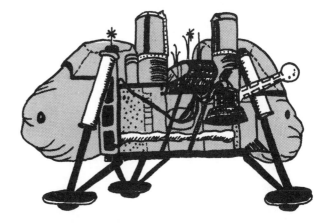

 Set:

Scientists have wondered for centuries about creatures from outer space. Could it be that space creatures really exist? No one knows for sure, but learning more about the planet Mars may help us find out.

Mars is about half the size of Earth. Scientists call Mars the "Red Planet" because of its rust-colored soil. The surface of Mars has mountains, canyons, craters, and channels. Most of the air is carbon dioxide. The polar ice caps are frozen carbon dioxide, which we call "dry ice."

Mars has 2 moons shaped like giant potatoes. The larger moon makes one revolution every 30 hours. The smaller moon zips around Mars every 7½ hours, rising and setting twice each day!

Mars has seasons like Earth, but each season is much longer. Our year is 365 days. A year on mars is 687 days—almost twice as long.

On Earth all living things need liquid water to survive. On Mars, all the water is frozen. Scientists did not believe there could be any known plants or animals on Mars.

In 1976, the United States sent an unmanned spacecraft to Mars. The Viking I landed on the surface of Mars in July 1976. It tested soil samples and sent information and pictures back to Earth. From this, scientists now believe there is no life on Mars, but even they are not sure. The Red Planet is still a mystery.

 Go:

1. Because of its rust color, scientists call Mars the _____ _____.

2. Mars is about (¼, ⅓, ½) the size of Earth.

3. Another name for frozen carbon dioxide is _____.

4. Viking I was a (spacecraft, astronaut, moon).

5. What does Mars have that are like giant potatoes? _____ _____

6. What word in the last sentence of the story means "a puzzle"? _____

Name _____

Your Trip Into Space

Welcome aboard! You are about to become the first child in space. You will be a passenger aboard a spacecraft. Try to imagine just what it will be like.

The rockets fire and you are pressed back into your seat as if a huge hand is squeezing down on you. As you leave Earth's atmosphere, you feel lighter. At the "zero gravity point," you are weightless. Any objects not strapped down float—even you!

Early astronauts ate food from tubes. You can eat almost anything as long as it's moist. Moist food, like pudding, sticks to your tray. Watch out for potato chips...dry foods float away in zero gravity.

After lunch, you prepare for a space walk outside the spacecraft. You put on a special suit. It has oxygen, a radio, earphones, and even air conditioning. Just in case, there is a safety line to keep you from floating away.

All this activity has made you tired. You can't just lie down. In zero gravity, there is no "down." Zip yourself into your sleeping bag attached to the wall. Don't forget to strap down your pillow so it doesn't float off while you're asleep.

Now read each question. Think about your adventure aboard the spacecraft. Write your best answer for each of the questions.

Choose two people to be your fellow astronauts and tell why you think each is a good choice.

_____

_____

_____

_____

What three things from Earth would you miss most and why?

_____

_____

_____

_____

Name _____

What would be the best part of your space flight?

_____

_____

_____

_____

What would be the worst part of your space flight?

_____

_____

_____

_____

Would you really volunteer to be the first child in space? Why or why not?

_____

_____

_____

_____

You wouldn't get me up in one of those things!

Space Crossword Puzzle

sun	moons	sky
constellation		star
eclipse		planets
meteor		sunlight
atmosphere		orbit
solar		satellite
comets		lunar

Use the word box to help you complete
the sentences and solve the puzzle.

Across:

1. The moon blocks our view of the sun in a solar _____.
4. There are nine _____ in our solar system.
6. Earth has one, but other planets have many _____.
7. The moon is the earth's natural _____.
8. The earth makes one _____ around the sun each year.
10. The sun is our closest _____.
11. Our _____ is the air surrounding our earth.

Down:

2. A _____ is a grouping of stars.
3. The energy from the sun that we can see is _____.
5. An eclipse of the sun is a _____ eclipse.
6. A shooting star is not really a star. It's a _____.
7. The _____ is the center of our solar system.
9. A _____ eclipse is an eclipse of the moon.

Name _____

How Many Moons?

MOONS!

Our earth has one moon. Mercury and Venus have no moons. The chart below shows the number of known moons for each of the other planets of our solar system. Use the chart to help you solve the problems.

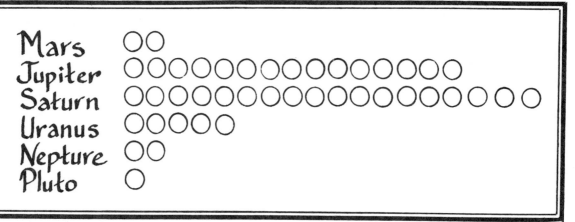

Mars   ○○
Jupiter   ○○○○○○○○○○○○○
Saturn   ○○○○○○○○○○○○○○○○○○○
Uranus   ○○○○○
Neptune   ○○
Pluto   ○

1. How many moons do Neptune and Uranus have together?

    1.   work space

2. How many more moons has Jupiter than Mars?

    2.

3. How many more moons has Saturn than Jupiter?

    3.

4. How many moons do Pluto and Mars have together?

    4.

Bonus: How many moons are in our solar system?

Name _____

Space Quick Check

 Use the word box to help you complete the sentences.

planets	moon	constellation	stars	solar
eclipse	satellite	meteors	lunar	sun

1. Our _____ is a star.

2. The _____ is a natural satellite of Earth.

3. There are nine planets in our _____ system.

4. Earth, Mars, Jupiter, and Pluto are _____.

5. Because of the earth's atmosphere, _____ appear to twinkle.

6. _____ are sometimes called shooting stars.

7. A group of stars may be called a _____.

 Write "Yes" for true, and write "No" for not true.

8. _____ Once people believed that the sun revolved around the earth.

9. _____ The world's first space traveler was a cat.

10. _____ A satellite is an object that revolves around a planet.

11. _____ Mars is called the Red Planet.

12. _____ All satellites are natural satellites.

13. _____ Neil Armstrong first stepped on the moon's surface in July 1969.

14. _____ Some planets have many moons.

★Bonus: _____

Do you think there really are space creatures?

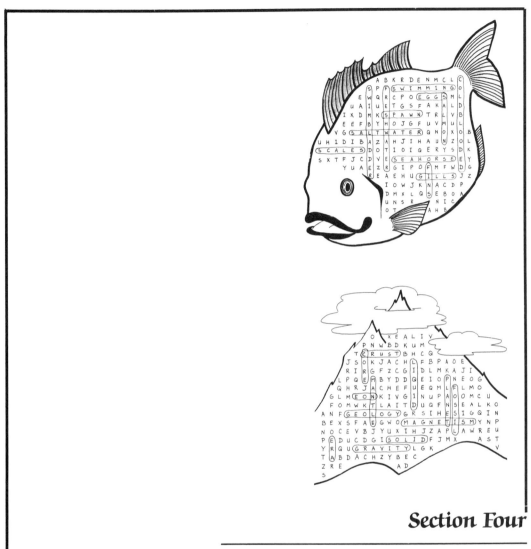

Section Four

ANSWER KEY

SECTION TWO: LIFE SCIENCE ACTIVITIES

SEEDS WORDS SEARCH

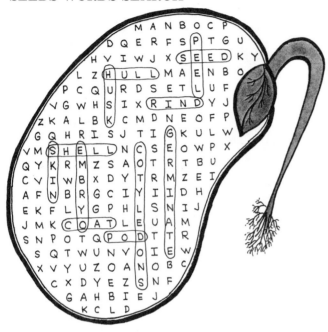

SEEDS

Answers will vary.

CORN AND BEANS

1. leaves
2. embryo
3. cotyledons
4. food
5. coat
6. roots

SPROUT LETTERS

4	1	6
3	2	5

ALL ABOUT VANILLA

Ready

1. aroma
2. product
3. rootlets
4. expensive
5. imitate
6. flavor

Go

1. cultivated
2. 3
3. 5, 10
4. seeds
5. yes
6. answers will vary
7. imitation

SEED DISTRIBUTION

1. a
2. different
3. scatter
4. move
5. on
6. dry
7. sea
8. float
9. fur
10. places

PLANT CROSSWORD PUZZLE

1. chlorophyll
2. water
3. transpiration
4. food
5. energy
6. nutrients
7. photosynthesis
8. oxygen
9. soil
10. minerals

PHOTOSYNTHESIS

1. sun
2. sugar, oxygen
3. leaves
4. roots

ALL ABOUT A VENUS' FLYTRAP

Ready

1. insects
2. gland
3. fluid
4. greenhouse
5. secrete
6. blade

Go

1. bog
2. nitrogen
3. 1
4. 2
5. no
6. no
7. withers

A TERRARIUM

1. means	6. terrarium
2. water	7. too
3. terrarium	8. wet
4. the	9. damp
5. young	10. grow

SEED PACKAGE MATH

1. $2.28	4. $2.44
2. $2.23	*Bonus:* $1.28
3. $2.14	

PLANT PARTS

1. plant	6. carry
2. important	7. because
3. soil	8. needs
4. needed	9. baby
5. like	10. big

ALL ABOUT ALOE-VERA

Ready

1. stalk	4. bitter
2. jagged	5. evaporation
3. rosette	6. red

Go

1. warm countries	5. bitter
2. rosette	6. pain
3. yellow, reddish	7. evaporation
4. violet	

MORE ABOUT PLANT PARTS

Definitions will vary.

| 1. flower | 3. roots |
| 2. leaves | 4. stem |

FLOWERS WORD SEARCH

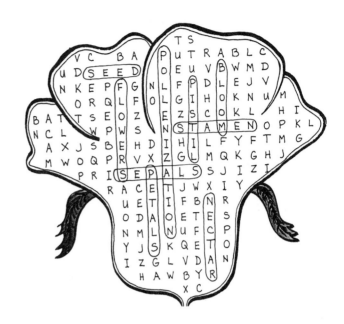

FLOWER PARTS

Definitions will vary.

1. stigma	6. pollen
2. pistil	7. anther
3. petal	8. stamen
4. ovary	9. pollen tube
5. seed	10. sepal

THE FLOWER

1. Earth	6. opens
2. Others	7. another
3. could	8. pollen
4. plant	9. tiny
5. color	10. seed

ALL ABOUT THE ARTICHOKE

Ready

1. prickly	4. divided
2. edible	5. thistle
3. related	6. sunflower

Go

1. flower bud
2. 2, 3
3. yes
4. sunflower
5. edible
6. marinated
7. transported

ALL ABOUT CHEWING GUM

Ready

1. collecting
2. purified
3. rubber
4. ingredients
5. pure
6. chicle

Go

1. sapodilla
2. chicle
3. peppermint, spearmint
4. automatic machines
5. 1860s
6. rubber
7. whirling

PLANT PRODUCTS

1. every
2. foods
3. woven
4. trees
5. rubber
6. leather
7. from
8. colors
9. make
10. plants

MORE ABOUT PLANT PRODUCTS
Answers will vary.

BEE'S SPECIALTY

1. blossom
2. roses
3. flower
4. nectar
5. rain
6. petals
7. sepals
8. seed
9. stamen
10. pistil
11. bloom
12. garden

Bonus: pollenization

PLANT GRAPH

1. Randi's
2. Ray
3. Candy, Glenn
4. 2 inches
5. 3 plants
6. 1 inch

PLANTS QUICK CHECK

1. seed
2. photosynthesis
3. flowers
4. water
5. chlorophyll
6. yes
7. yes
8. yes
9. no
10. no
11. yes
12. yes

INSECT CHARACTERISTICS
Definitions will vary.

AN INSECT'S BODY

1. wing
2. thorax
3. head
4. abdomen
5. antenna
6. mouth
7. leg

ALL ABOUT SPIDERS

Ready

1. cocoon
2. spinnerets
3. snare
4. prey
5. survive

Go

1. 2
2. spiders
3. yes
4. spinnerets
5. hand
6. 20
7. cocoon
8. molt

THE MONARCH

1. produces
2. taste
3. butterfly
4. return
5. tiny
6. growing
7. twig
8. Now
9. open
10. dry

AN ANT HOUSE

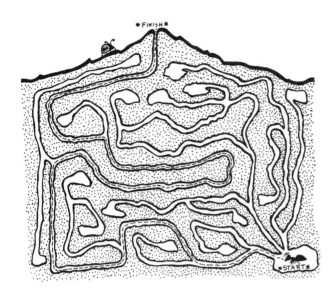

WHAT'S A BIRD?

1. no	6. no
2. yes	7. yes
3. yes	8. no
4. yes	9. no
5. no	10. yes

EGGS, EGGS, EGGS

1. yellow	6. Every
2. around	7. days
3. hard	8. small
4. inside	9. hours
5. chick	10. feathers

BEAKS AND FEET

7, 6, 1, 2, 5, 4, 9, 8, 3

ALL ABOUT THE EMPEROR

Ready

1. belly	4. marine
2. waterproof	5. rookeries
3. protect	6. blubber

Go

1. rookery	4. crèche
2. 4	5. 6
3. yes	6. no

MIRANDA'S EGGS

1. 55 eggs	4. 80 eggs
2. 42 eggs	*Bonus:* 169 eggs, 845 eggs
3. 72 eggs	

SEA TURTLES

1. these	6. balls
2. swim	7. ocean
3. flippers	8. baby
4. tired	9. beach
5. deep	10. water

REPTILES AND AMPHIBIANS

1. A	5. R, A
2. R	6. A
3. R	7. A
4. R, A	8. R, A

WHICH IS IT?

frog—amphibian	lizard—reptile
turtle—reptile	snake—reptile
salamander—amphibian	

ALL ABOUT ALLIGATORS AND CROCODILES

Ready

1. heavy	4. cigar-shaped
2. submerged	5. blunt
3. snout	6. powerful

Go

1. yes	4. no
2. tails	5. eyes, nostrils
3. snouts	5. larger

ALL ABOUT SNAKES

Ready

1. environment
2. prey
3. backbone
4. temperature
5. grip
6. reptiles

Go

1. eggs
2. tongues
3. 300
4. no
5. yes
6. hear

A FISHY WORD SEARCH

SEAHORSES

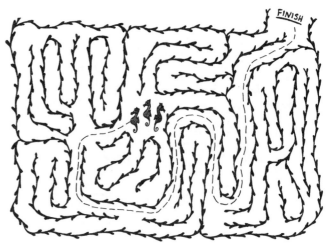

WHAT IS A FISH?

1. yes
2. yes
3. yes
4. no
5. yes
6. no

A FISH'S BODY

1. fins
2. swim bladder
3. gills
4. eye
5. head
6. body
7. tail
8. scales

ALL ABOUT SALMON

Ready

1. mysterious
2. redd
3. bruised
4. spawn
5. alevins
6. rapids

Go

1. yes
2. alevins
3. no
4. fish ladders
5. female

THE DERBY

1. Chris
2. 3 pounds, 8 ounces
3. Lee
4. 3 pounds, 8 ounces
5. Toni

Bonus: 2nd, 4th, 5th, 3rd, 1st

216

HOW'S THE WEATHER?

1. sees
2. knows
3. hibernate
4. member
5. teeth
6. of
7. adult
8. burrows
9. den
10. hear

MAMMALS

1. no
2. yes
3. no
4. yes
5. no
6. yes

WHICH MAMMAL GROUP?

1. hoofed animals
2. primates
3. carnivores
4. rodents
5. marsupials
6. marine mammals

ALL ABOUT THE PLATYPUS

Ready
1. roots
2. similar
3. burrow
4. winding
5. ooze

Go
1. mammal
2. Australia, Tasmania
3. lay eggs
4. no
5. 60
6. feet, bills

ALL ABOUT CHIMPANZEES

Ready
1. task
2. grasp
3. upright
4. knuckle
5. communicate
6. imitate

Go
1. man
2. yes
3. termite stick
4. colors
5. primates

MATCH THE CRITTERS!

rodent—squirrel
hoofed animals—pig
carnivores—fox
marine mammals—dolphin
marsupial—kangaroo
primate—baboon

KILLER WHALES

1. about
2. easy
3. white
4. more
5. feet
6. teeth
7. groups
8. whales
9. other
10. stayed

ANIMAL FAMILIES

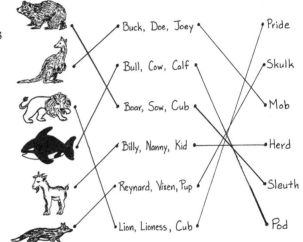

THE GREAT RACE

1. Hare, Ostrich
2. 20 mph
3. no
4. 15 mph
5. Snake
6. Eagle
7. Duck

ANIMALS QUICK CHECK

1. milk
2. feathers
3. reptiles
4. hair
5. land
6. gills
7. air
8. yes
9. no
10. no
11. yes
12. no
13. yes
14. yes
15. no

BONES AND MUSCLES WORD SEARCH

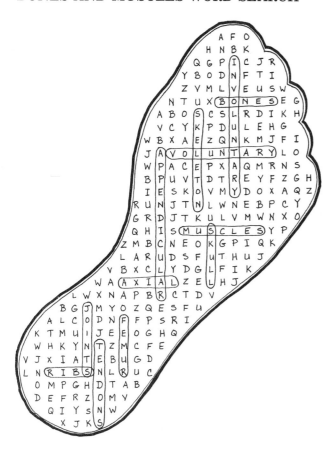

YOUR BODY'S FRAMEWORK

1. bones
2. and
3. heart
4. neck
5. are
6. to
7. make
8. inside
9. bone
10. think

MUSCLES AND TENDONS

1. smooth
2. skeletal
3. heart
4. I
5. V
6. I
7. I
8. V
9. V
10. V
11. V

LABEL THE BONES, TENDONS, AND MUSCLES

1. bone
2. muscle
3. tendon
4. tendon
5. muscle
6. bone

THE BELLOWS

1. body
2. your
3. nose
4. and
5. or
6. tube
7. air
8. called
9. are
10. ribs

JUST YOUR TYPE

Ready

1. quart
2. waste
3. donor
4. liquid
5. recipient

Go

1. plasma
2. Dr. Karl Landsteiner
3. A, B, AB, O
4. yes
5. 0
6. platelets

YOUR BRAIN

1. forebrain; answers will vary
2. midbrain; answers will vary
3. hindbrain; answers will vary

PARTS OF THE BRAIN

1. Brain Stem
2. Cerebrum
3. Cerebellum

EYES

1. yes
2. no
3. yes
4. yes
5. no
6. no
7. yes
8. yes

PARTS OF THE EYE

1. eyebrow   5. pupil
2. eyelid   6. sclera
3. eyelash   7. tear duct
4. iris   8. cornea

MMM . . . YUK!

1. nerve   6. sense
2. taste   7. at
3. cells   8. mouth
4. they   9. than
5. tongue   10. else

THE FIVE SENSES

Answers will vary.

MORE THAN JUST SOUND

1. also   6. brain
2. is   7. messages
3. parts   8. nerves
4. and   9. head
5. filled   10. spins

FINGERPRINTS

Answers will vary.

ALL ABOUT YOUR BODY'S OUTER COAT

Ready
1. sole   4. moist
2. sweat   5. follicles
3. epidermis 6. palm

Go
1. 2   4. 2
2. epidermis, dermis   5. dermis
3. no   6. oil

ALL ABOUT GERMS

Ready
1. disease
2. century
3. germs
4. antibiotics
5. split

Go
1. germs   5. viruses
2. yes   6. evil spirits
3. bacteria   7. antibiotics
4. bacteria

WHY GET SHOTS?!

1. shots   6. injected
2. get   7. you
3. that   8. kinds
4. shot   9. other
5. very   10. they

HOW DO YOU MEASURE UP?

Answers will vary.

HUMAN BODY QUICK CHECK

1. skeleton   9. yes
2. tendons   10. no
3. muscles   11. no
4. lungs   12. yes
5. heart   13. yes
6. blood   14. yes
7. brain   15. yes
8. no

SECTION THREE:
EARTH SCIENCE ACTIVITIES

GEOLOGY WORD SEARCH

HOW BIG IS SMALL?

1. water	6. planet
2. earth	7. about
3. people	8. around
4. It	9. through
5. the	10. dig

CRUST, MANTLE, CORE

1. no	6. no
2. yes	7. yes
3. no	8. yes
4. yes	9. no
5. yes	10. yes

PARTS OF THE EARTH

1. atmosphere	3. mantle
2. crust	4. core

ALL ABOUT MAGNETISM

Ready

1. equator	4. century
2. magical	5. opposite
3. attracted	6. rotates

Go

1. 2,000	4. magnetic field
2. lodestones	5. poles
3. compass	6. earth

MYSTERIOUS GRAVITY

1. pulls	6. pounds
2. earth	7. are
3. see	8. far
4. gravity	9. have
5. pulls	10. weigh

ANCIENT PRINTS

1. ancient	6. mud
2. are	7. layers
3. find	8. rock
4. years	9. deep
5. lakes	10. the

THE EARTH'S STORY

Answers will vary.

THE PHANEROZOIC EON

1. yes
2. yes
3. no
4. no
5. yes

ALL ABOUT RADIOCARBONS

Ready

1. rays, decays
2. archaeologist
3. prehistoric
4. radioactive
5. creatures
6. remaining

Go

1. rays
2. absorb
3. yes
4. one-half
5. old

NAME IT!

1. Stegosaurus
2. 150 million
3. Stegosaurus
4. 20 feet
5. 5 tons
6. plants

HOW MUCH DO YOU WEIGH?

1. 71 pounds
2. 8 pounds
3. the sun
4. the moon
5. Saturn
6. 3
7. 2

A ROCK STORY

1. rocks
2. just
3. kind
4. means
5. and
6. are
7. years
8. found
9. rocks
10. changed

WHAT MAKES MOUNTAINS?

Answers will vary.

MORE ABOUT MOUNTAINS

1. Forces pushed upward and sideways to form folds in the earth's crust.
2. The earth's crust was broken into blocks.

More About Mountains (con't)

3. Molten rock spread out in layers under the earth's surface.
4. Volcanoes erupted through a crack in the earth's crust.

5.

6. Answers will vary.
7. Answers will vary.

ALL ABOUT MOUNT ST. HELENS

Ready

1. approximately
2. pyroclastic
3. tremors
4. mudflow
5. spurts
6. perish
7. bulge

Go

1. 123 years
2. vanished
3. yes
4. Washington
5. record
6. yes

VOLCANOES

1. inside
2. rock
3. surface
4. has
5. from
6. eruption
7. called
8. volcanoes
9. erupt
10. very

GEYSERS

1. both
2. shoots
3. crust
4. pressure
5. air
6. geyser
7. because
8. eruption
9. water
10. geyser

ALL ABOUT RIVERS OF ICE

Ready

1. flow
2. ancient
3. scooping
4. erode
5. compact
6. glacier

Go

1. valley glacier
2. yes
3. ice
4. Antarctica
5. no
6. temperature

EARTHQUAKES

1. ground
2. it
3. pressure
4. stick
5. earth
6. crust
7. called
8. waves
9. seismic
10. earthquakes

MOUNT EVEREST MAZE

HOW HIGH?

1. 20,320 feet
2. South Dakota
3. Mount Logan and Mount McKinley
4. 13,680 feet
5. Pikes Peak
6. 5

Bonus: Mount Logan

GEOLOGY QUICK CHECK

1. sphere
2. metal
3. fossils
4. crust
5. gravity
6. mantle
7. glacier
8. yes
9. no
10. yes
11. yes
12. no
13. no
14. yes
15. yes

WHAT MAKES WEATHER?

1. days
2. cool
3. hours
4. only
5. weather
6. earth
7. is
8. more
9. from
10. sun

ALL ABOUT HURRICANES AND TORNADOES

Ready

1. equator
2. homeless
3. funnel
4. enormous
5. recent
6. forecaster

Go

1. water
2. eye
3. hurricane, tornado
4. 600
5. yes
6. 400

MORE THAN JUST WATER

1. water	6. become
2. filled	7. frozen
3. together	8. again
4. heavy	9. formed
5. fall	10. water

THUNDER AND LIGHTNING

1. thunderstorms	6. quickly
2. year	7. thunder
3. called	8. how
4. air	9. hearing
5. ice	10. lightning

THE WATER CYCLE

1. sun	5. run-off
2. three	6. vapor
3. precipitation	7. condensation
4. amount	8. living

ALL ABOUT CLOUDS

Ready

1. hazy	4. nimbus
2. predict	5. wispy
3. drizzly	

Go

1. Luke Howard	4. cirrus
2. cumulus	5. yes
3. stratus	6. predict

WEATHER OR CLIMATE?

Answers will vary.

LOST IN THE CLOUDS

WEATHER WORD SEARCH

223

FORECASTING TOOLS

1. anemometer or wind gauge
2. wind speed
3. camera
4. cloud patterns
5. rain gauge
6. rainfall
7. thermometer
8. air temperature
9. hygrometer
10. moisture or humidity

MAPPING THE WEATHER

1. foggy
2. no, too cold
3. east
4. no
6. Atlanta
7. Miami
8. Fort Worth
9. Chicago

BREEZE OR GALE?

1. ○⟍⟍
2. small trees
3. moderate breeze
4. 25-31 mph
5. 6
6. ○⟍⟍⟍
7. calm
8. 0 mph
9. straight up

ALL ABOUT WEATHER RHYMES

Ready
1. forecast, predict
2. agree
3. instruments
4. crackling
5. simple

Go
1. ending
2. instruments
3. ice
4. no
5. farmers
6. no

ALL ABOUT WEATHER MYTHS

Ready
1. legend, myth
2. swallows
3. migrate
4. hibernation
5. common
6. calendar

Go
1. legend
2. groundhog
3. 6
4. California
5. no
6. migrate

GRADE THE FORECASTER
Answers will vary.

A "HAIRY" HYGROMETER
4 1 3
6 5 2

HIGHS AND LOWS

1. 5°
2. 20°
3. 24°
4. 20°
5. 31°
6. 4°
7. 15°
8. 8°

Bonus: Miami, Los Angeles, Houston, Denver, Chicago, New York, Washington, Anchorage

WEATHER QUICK CHECK

1. precipitation
2. cycle
3. tornadoes
4. thunder
5. climate
6. evaporates
7. yes
8. yes
9. no
10. no
11. yes
12. no
13. no

THE SUN

1. because   6. Its
2. miles   7. could
3. sun   8. sun
4. faster   9. different
5. largest   10. dark

PHASES OF THE MOON
4, 5, 2, 1, 3

A NATURAL SATELLITE

1. smaller   6. ball
2. pounds   7. called
3. light   8. are
4. water   9. around
5. moon   10. earth

TWINKLE, TWINKLE

1. star   6. see
2. than   7. atmosphere
3. larger   8. them
4. stars   9. made
5. are   10. stars

ALL ABOUT AN ECLIPSE

Ready
1. evil   4. partial
2. visible   5. solar
3. lunar   6. ancient

Go
1. dragon   4. every 18 years
2. solar   5. sun, moon, and earth
3. lunar   6. 7

FAMILY OF PLANETS

1. MERCURY   9. PLUTO
2. VENUS   10. yes
3. EARTH   11. no
4. MARS   12. no
5. JUPITER   13. yes
6. SATURN   14. no
7. URANUS   15. no
8. NEPTUNE   16. yes

ALL ABOUT SHOOTING STARS

Ready
1. famous   4. streak
2. survives   5. atmosphere
3. crater   6. occasional

Go
1. no   4. yes
2. dirty   5. crater
3. more

THE SKY DRAGON

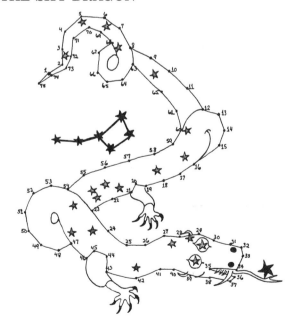

SPACE WORD SEARCH

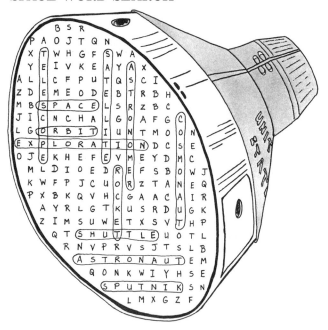

ALL ABOUT EARLY ASTRONOMERS

Ready
1. astronomer
2. punished
3. satellite
4. motionless
5. severe

Go
1. earth
2. telescope
3. prison
4. sun
5. yes

SATELLITES

1. weigh
2. Earth
3. space
4. around
5. orbit
6. too
7. gravity
8. the
9. into
10. and

ANIMAL ASTRONAUTS

1. rode
2. very
3. was
4. body
5. inside
6. animals
7. and
8. space
9. living
10. animal

ALL ABOUT FOOTPRINTS ON THE MOON

Ready
1. astronaut
2. rod
3. gravity
4. crew
5. surface

Go
1. 2
2. no
3. answers may include scooped up rocks, took pictures, displayed the flag
4. July 20, 1969
5. There is no wind nor rain on the moon
6. President Richard Nixon

MAN IN SPACE

1. Sputnik—1957
2. Men in space—1961
3. US orbits Earth—1962
4. Woman in space—1963
5. Walk in space—1965
6. Soft moon landing—1966
7. Moon footprints—1969
8. Space shuttle—1981

ALL ABOUT MARS

Ready
1. rust
2. seasons
3. century
4. soil
5. liquid
6. channel

Go
1. Red Planet
2. ½
3. dry ice
4. spacecraft
5. 2 moons
6. mystery

YOUR TRIP INTO SPACE
Answers will vary.

SPACE CROSSWORD PUZZLE

Across

1. eclipse	8. orbit
4. planets	10. star
6. moons	11. atmosphere
7. satellite	

Down

2. constellation	6. meteor
3. sunlight	7. sun
5. solar	9. lunar

HOW MANY MOONS?

1. 7
2. 13
3. 3
4. 3
Bonus: 43

SPACE QUICK CHECK

1. sun	8. yes
2. moon	9. no
3. solar	10. yes
4. planets	11. yes
5. stars	12. no
6. meteors	13. yes
7. constellation	14. yes